Passport to Shame

# PASSPORT
## TO SHAME

## From Asian Immigrant
## to American Addict

Sam Louie, MA, LMHC

CRP®
CENTRAL RECOVERY PRESS
LAS VEGAS

**Central Recovery Press** (CRP) is committed to publishing exceptional materials addressing addiction treatment, recovery, and behavioral healthcare topics.

For more information, visit www.centralrecoverypress.com.

28 27 26 25 24 23     1 2 3 4 5

*Library of Congress Cataloging-in-Publication Data*

Names: Louie, Sam, author.
Title: Passport to shame : from Asian immigrant to American addict / Sam
  Louie.
Description: Las Vegas, NV : Central Recovery Press, 2022. | Summary: "A
  psychotherapist's candid memoir of addiction and recovery, exploring the
  intersection of Asian culture, mental health, and assimilating into
  American culture as an ethnic minority"-- Provided by publisher.
Identifiers: LCCN 2022041462 (print) | LCCN 2022041463 (ebook) | ISBN
  9781949481686 (paperback) | ISBN 9781949481693 (ebook)
Subjects: LCSH: Louie, Sam. | Psychotherapists--United States--Biography. |
  Chinese Americans--Biography. | Sex addicts--United States--Biography. |
  Television journalists--United States--Biography.
Classification: LCC RC438.6.L68 A3 2022  (print) | LCC RC438.6.L68  (ebook)
  | DDC 616.89/14092 [B]--dc23/eng/20221003
LC record available at https://lccn.loc.gov/2022041462
LC ebook record available at https://lccn.loc.gov/2022041463

Photos are from the author's personal collection.

*Cover and interior design by Sara Streifel, Think Creative Design*

# CONTENTS

# Introduction

*"So ashamed that the ancestors*
*of eight generations can even feel it."*

CHINESE PROVERB

Asian cultures are rooted in shame. They are known as shame-based societies because the lives, families, and mindsets of these cultures revolve around some aspect of avoiding shame to preserve familial and cultural honor. In Chinese culture alone, there are more than 100 different ways to describe shame. While some of them overlap with English versions of shame, such as a sense of disgrace and humiliation, many others help shed light on why and how shame is so pertinent among Asian cultures. Within the Chinese, some of the shame-related terms and references are: *a nation's humiliation/shame* (i.e. bringing shame to yourself also brings shame to your family, ancestors, and community and your entire ethnic background and/or family's country of origin); *the old father-in-law carries the young daughter-in-law on his back to cross a river* (in Chinese culture, it is considered inappropriate for a father-in-law to have physical contact with his daughter-in-law, thus equating how taboo it is to be associated with shame); and *a person lives by face as much as a tree lives by bark and as much as a light bulb is covered with glass* (i.e. stressing the importance of maintaining a positive and good-standing public image).

To encourage conformity, shame is built into child-rearing practices. Asian children are shamed early on as a means of guiding social and moral behaviors. In addition to collectivism, religions and philosophies such as Buddhism and Confucianism perpetuate shame, as they value filial piety, obedience, authority, ancestral worship, and loyalty to family. In other words, to let others down simply by deviating from social or family norms or engaging in behaviors that can be seen as shameful is much more negatively impactful to Asians than Westerners.

In Asian culture, shame often begins early. Basic human needs such as touching, relationships, and affirmation can be thwarted during this time. When primary caregivers do not display physical signs of affection like hugs or kisses, verbal affirmation such as words of encouragement, or take the time to know their children individually, these children may develop internal core messages: "I'm not good enough," "I'm not loveable," "I'm a bad person."

Shame is powerful. Children and adults will do anything to thwart those feelings. Some become perfectionists or try to prove their worth through academics, sports, or careers. Others may become susceptible to addictions, seeking to fill their core emotional needs in unhealthy ways (drugs, alcohol, food, gambling, shopping, work, sex, etc.).

Unlike the United States and other Western countries, which pride themselves on individualism, equality, and autonomy, traditional Asian nations exalt collectivism, hierarchy, and obedience. As a result, Asian societies are often referred to as "shame-based cultures," in which social order is maintained through the use of shame. Identities are forged by upholding honor while avoiding any shame-producing feelings, thoughts, beliefs, or behaviors. This presents a cultural bind where the shame leads those to suffer in silence, since acknowledgement can be met with family, community, and cultural rejection, ostracism, or banishment.

I should know. My life was once shackled by shame. As a first-generation Chinese immigrant to the United States, I was challenged by shame from the moment I arrived on these shores. The shame of being Asian in America, the shame of prejudice and racism, the shame of Asian masculinity, the shame of breaking away from Asian norms, and eventually the shame of my addiction. Not just my addiction but a family legacy of addiction.

I come from at least three generations of addicts. My grandparents were compulsive gamblers. My uncles and aunts also gamble. Some of my relatives struggled with infidelity. My parents were workaholics. My brothers struggled with their own compulsive and addictive tendencies. And I inherited a combination of the above addictions, in addition to carrying the burden to be the first in my lineage to succeed in America. The burden of hidden shame and addictions was immense until it was finally lifted. I've accepted and overcome the shame and also tried to be of service to those still suffering from it. I hope this book will help you do the same, by encouraging you to courageously explore your past and pain, knowing that by doing so you can still bring honor to your heritage and yourself.

PART I

# The Asian Immigrant

# The Departure

I hate myself!

This was one of my earliest thoughts as a Chinese boy in the United States. I wasn't white like those I saw on television. I wasn't Black like those in my neighborhood. I was an Asian immigrant. I was an outsider, a foreigner, the "other." It was 1976 and I was four years old. I hated looking different, speaking different, and having different customs and traditions from mainstream America.

In Hong Kong, we were part of the Cantonese-speaking Chinese majority. I never felt different there. Hong Kong was not only home to my parents but also my grandparents, great-grandparents, and their ancestors. Cantonese is the largest Chinese dialect in Hong Kong, Macau, and parts of Southeastern China.

Hong Kong was a British colony from 1842 until the handover back to China in 1997. For myself, this meant my early identity and roots were a confluence of British and Chinese. I can still recall the juxtaposition of British double-decker buses with traditional Chinese fishing "junks" along the Hong Kong harbor. Additionally, I have memories of our British passports to mark our distinction as Chinese with British citizenship, so even before setting foot in America I was ethnically Chinese but legally British. My young mind thought it was cool that I could be both Chinese and British. But this all changed when my parents decided to move the family to America. The first English words I heard were, "Ching, chong, chong!" Not exactly the most welcoming reception. The first question hurled our way was whether we ate rats or dogs. I cringed and began distancing myself from my Chinese background.

This cultural contempt and self-loathing became evident when my parents spoke to me and my brothers in Chinese and I responded in English. I was embarrassed and ashamed of our heritage. I winced when they spoke Chinese in public. I wanted nothing to do with them in any setting, public or private.

The shame of my native tongue couldn't have been more pronounced than when I was stuck in an enclosed city bus with my grandmother. During the weekends, while my parents worked, our grandmother watched over me and my brothers. She would ride the bus to Seattle's Chinatown to get groceries and I'd come along just to break the monotony. My grandmother was also hard of hearing, so she shouted when speaking Chinese. It felt as if all eyes were on us, listening with suspicion to the most foreign of sounds to ever land on their ears. To ease the perceived tension, I did my best to respond in perfect English, thinking that by doing so everyone would view me as a legitimate American.

But it didn't matter if I could speak English without an accent, because there was no way I could get rid of my skin tone. It wasn't for a lack of effort, though. There were times when I took a bar of soap and scrubbed it hard against my flesh, hoping it would turn lighter. Obviously, that didn't help. I would have to live with my skin tone, a dead giveaway that no matter where I went I could always be singled out, targeted, and labeled as the foreigner.

## The Oldest Son of the Oldest Son

The tension of growing up in a Western, individualistic society while living in a collectivist household was not lost on me. I was told time and again by my parents and other relatives that my life was to represent and honor my family and Chinese heritage. Individual pursuits and ideas were to be ignored, no matter what mainstream society was telling me. The weight of these expectations impacted me disproportionately, as I was the oldest son of the oldest son.

My father is the oldest son of seven children. My grandparents on my dad's side were in an arranged marriage and it showed. Issues of domestic violence, gambling, and strife plagued their relationship and impacted the family. I'm told my grandfather had a gambling problem and eventually abandoned the family and moved from Hong Kong to Australia for a number of years, while my dad was tasked to work to help support the family. He dropped out of school by the time he was thirteen and began working in Chinese restaurants.

Along the way, he met a waitress who would become his wife (my mother). By the age of thirty, my father had risen to the rank of chef and was making a name for himself. Yet, with three toddlers in tow, his individual aspirations were set aside for the desires of the family. My parents wanted a better opportunity for us. Neither of them had much of an education, as both came from poverty.

The Pacific Northwest became their destination when a restaurant near Seattle wanted to sponsor my dad to work in the United States. Based on what they had heard about America, my parents felt it was in the collective best interest to move here. I say "collective" because not only did this mean our nuclear family could immigrate to the U.S., but so could my grandparents, aunts, and uncles due to the immigration policies of that time. Thus, one fateful day in the summer of 1976, everyone on my dad's side of the family packed a suitcase and flew to Seattle to start life anew.

## From Majority to Minority

When my parents left Hong Kong to immigrate to the United States, it was for a better future for me and my two younger brothers. It was not an easy decision, as they were already in their early thirties, but they forged ahead, thinking their sacrifice would be worth it so we could receive an American education.

My parents were part of the dominant culture in Hong Kong and viewed life through that prism of ethnic and cultural privilege. They were not only illiterate immigrants to a new land but an ethnic minority popularized in Hollywood as strange, exotic, and foreign. My father worked as a chef for a Chinese restaurant in the suburbs outside of Seattle and my mom was a waitress at a restaurant in Chinatown. Both worked long hours for low wages with no benefits. They didn't have medical or dental insurance. There was no paid sick leave or vacation.

Beyond the cultural shock of adjusting to a new language and customs, they were stripped of the status of being part of the majority. Not only were they known as Chinese immigrants, they were a minority living in a Black community. My family struggled to make sense of our place in this new land.

The Seattle zip code of 98118 where we grew up is now one of the most ethnically diverse in the United States, with speakers of fifty-nine languages. However, when we arrived in the neighborhood, it was predominantly African-American with a growing population of Chinese, Japanese, and Filipinos.

People may erroneously view culture shock as the simplistic process of assimilating into traditional, mainstream white society. For us, we had the additional layer of trying to navigate and integrate into an African-American community. I point this out because growing up in a Black neighborhood helped shape part of my identity. Hobbies, sports, music, and the culture of Black America were adopted as my own. I viewed life through the prism of three lenses: mainstream white America, Asian, and Black.

When it comes to the perception of Asian identity, one big misconception people have is to clump us into a large, all-encompassing, monolithic group with scant understanding of the various ethnic, cultural, religious, and linguistic differences that set us apart. They also fail to recognize the different American cultural influences that impact our sense of self. Our identity is much more than our ethnicity. It includes the subcultures we experienced growing up.

In addition, the values of Asian collectivism and groupthink that my parents and other relatives tried to impress on me and my brothers clashed with American ideals of independence. We were being taught at school to speak up, question authority, and think critically, while at home our parents stressed the importance of obedience, harmony, and never questioning authority figures like teachers, elders, and parents.

How would all of this impact our sense of identity and shape how others viewed us or how we saw ourselves?

Regardless of which type of community you grew up in, this belief that you are different from mainstream society becomes the first aspect of life many Asians encounter. The teasing, taunts, and racial slurs remind us that we are foreign, different, and at times considered un-American. The common caricatures associated with being Asian came my way starting in kindergarten. Questions like "Where are you really from?" were commonplace. These questions, while sometimes benign and not meant to be cruel, nevertheless reaffirmed to my young mind that I was different and less than American. Something needed to change quickly if I was going to fit in.

## A 'Nice' American Name

My Chinese first name, Fu Yuen, was another reminder of my foreignness. At school, I shuddered when teachers gave roll call and said my first name. I dreaded this ritual. I could hear kids snickering, so I feigned indifference, but the truth was it hurt.

Then one fateful day our parents decided to give us new names. They knew a white couple and asked them for "three nice American names" for me and my brothers. Without hesitation, the couple responded, "How about Sam, Ken, and Fred?" In one fell swoop, our Chinese names of Fu Yuen, Fu Kuen, and Fu Yueng were replaced with Sam, Ken, and Fred. We didn't have any say in the matter, as our parents thought this would be the best way to help us assimilate.

Despite the name change, teachers seemed to avoid my English name and gravitate toward my Chinese name, even though Sam was clearly written on the attendance sheets. They would fumble with the pronunciation of Fu Yuen and I'd quickly interject and say, "It's Sam!" This abandonment and embarrassment of my Chinese name is a sad aspect of assimilation. My mother also changed her name from Fung Ning to Fran. My father is the only one who kept his Chinese name, Wai Wan.

This abandonment of our birth names to fit into mainstream society struck me as a paradox later in life, when I learned American expatriates who live overseas don't consider changing their names to assimilate. Changing our names was viewed favorably as a gesture of our willingness to adopt and adapt to American norms. Those who didn't would be viewed more harshly. Nevertheless, there were those who kept their ethnic names, but it came with the risk of being teased by other kids, of not getting called back for job interviews, and of feeling further alienated from mainstream society.

Historically, being forced to change one's name is about power and control. Think about the slaves from Africa who were stripped of all their rights and their names. The TV miniseries *Roots* that aired in the 1970s is a reminder of how much a name meant, when the African slave who went by Kunta Kinte refused to accept his slave name "Toby." He eventually does accept it, but fiercely preserves his real name by reminding his descendants of it, along with the associated meaning, heritage, and pride that came with it.

Due to the oppression of slavery and Jim Crow laws, I can see why African-Americans today take pride in their ethnic names. I appreciate their desire to find a means to reconnect with their heritage. When you have to disown a major aspect of your identity, such as your name, to fit into American society, it feels like you're cutting off a part of yourself. Why are we asked to sacrifice so much to be accepted in this country? A country that presumably extols the virtues of diversity, yet at the same time shuns those who appear or sound too ethnic? While my new name served its purpose in helping me assimilate, there's also a sense of cultural abandonment. I haven't thought about reclaiming my Chinese name, but I have renounced the need to cater to what mainstream America wants me to be. I can stand proud to be an Asian-American, an American with a past that's different from the first European settlers.

## I Pledge Allegiance to My Family Name

In an Asian family, you learn honor early on, when your parents tell you about the meaning of your family name and its implications for your life. As a Louie, my honor, loyalty, and allegiance belonged to the family. What was important in life was not my individual self or accomplishments; everything I did was to be geared toward bringing glory to the family name.

Chinese names are written in three characters, with your family name first, not last. My Chinese name is Louie Fu Yuen. My father sat me down when I was three years old and helped me write my name. He circled the Louie character and emphasized that, "Fu Yuen doesn't matter much in life. What matters most is making sure you do good for the Louie name."

Traditionally, when Chinese people greet each other, what they really want to know beyond the normal pleasantries is one's family name. While your first name is needed, what's vital is knowing your last name, so they can understand you within the larger and richer context of your family's heritage. Both parties respond with their family name; this allows them to get a mutual sense of who they are based on a family's lineage and reputation. As a Louie, my reputation today is still impacted by the actions of my deceased ancestors.

## Guns, Crime, and Violence

Around the same time that I adopted Sam as my new name, I became aware and sensitive to the crime around me. My mother always picked me up from school, but one day when I was in the first grade an uncle did. I immediately sensed something was wrong. When I asked what happened, he told me someone tried to attack my mom at our family home. My heart stopped and time stood still. In age-appropriate language, my uncle conveyed that someone tried to rape my mom by posing as a city utility employee. My uncle shared that my mom was able to escape and run to the mini-mart at the top of our street and call for help. That day altered my understanding of safety. Our home was no longer safe. Our father worked and didn't return until we were already asleep. As the oldest male in the house, I took on the role of protector of the family to ensure this never happened again.

When I was in elementary school, someone tried to break into our house and my mother gathered me and my brothers in her bedroom, locked the doors, and shut off all the lights. I didn't understand the logic of staying silent while waiting for the police. In addition to calling the police, I called my best friend and told his family to come over. By the time police arrived, the robber had left, but the reality of living in an unsafe neighborhood was firmly established. I convinced an older friend to give me a BB gun for protection. I hid it under my bed and was hyper-vigilant of my surroundings. I would consistently peek out the windows of our backyard and survey the front yard for any possible signs of danger. As a reminder of the dangers around us, South Seattle was often in the local news because of shootings, robberies, and murders. Consequently, I became a light sleeper, ever on guard should I need to wake and fight off intruders. It was not lost on me that the homes in our neighborhood had windows with bars on them. People owned German shepherds and other loud, aggressive dogs to ward off burglars. Our neighborhood was highlighted in the news as a "dangerous" place.

Due to the crime, our parents had negative views of African-Americans. Additionally, there is a Chinese prejudice against Black people, as the Chinese word "haakgwai," which means "black ghost," was used when referring to African-Americans. My parents would discourage me from hanging out with Black friends and instead try to steer me toward other Asians. When I would use my money to buy my Black friends candy or comic books, it made them even angrier and they would tell me, "Black people can't be trusted!"

## I Want My Thanksgiving Turkey!

Because my parents were rooted in Asian worldviews about life and culture, they had no understanding of Western customs, holidays, or traditions. For example, on Thanksgiving, while I yearned to eat turkey with mashed potatoes, gravy, and cranberry sauce, my parents made us eat Peking duck instead. While there's no doubt the taste of Peking duck is succulent, my brothers and I clamored for years for a traditional Thanksgiving dinner. Yet year after year my parents resisted, finally relenting when I was eighteen years old, but by then I didn't care anymore.

Christmas, though, was a special holiday that I did care about, no matter how old I was. I yearned for the festive lights, wreaths, trees, and other symbols I saw in movies, on television, and at other friends's homes. But my parents didn't see it as practical to spend money on these things, so I went my entire childhood without them. One year a neighbor gave us an extra tree, but after experiencing the smell of pine needles in our home, the hope of more to come was quickly dashed when my mom said, "No more tree! Tree make too much mess!"

When it came to gifts, I wanted real ones with some thought behind them. Yet, in our family's tradition, instead of gifts our parents and extended family gave out Chinese red envelopes filled with money. To me, this felt like an easy way out. No thought was given to who I was as a person or to invest in gifts that could expand our horizons or nurture our interests. One uncle did break the mold by buying me various gifts over the years that I can still recall vividly: a juggling-ball set, a beginner's stamp-collector kit that made me curious about the wider world I was a part of, and a hacky sack (which I wasn't very good at). The point is this uncle tried to find gifts that would spur us toward learning, creativity, and growth.

Other areas of folklore that stood out included my parents's lack of understanding about the tooth fairy. I was in elementary school when I told my mom I was going to put my recently removed tooth under the pillow, and she just thought it was such an odd thing to do. When I shared gleefully about the tooth fairy coming overnight with money, she looked at me perplexed. Reality hit me the next day when I learned the hard way there was no tooth fairy.

## I Was Not 'Born in the U.S.A.'

Despite my Asian background, a part of me thought I was just as American as a white kid growing up in the suburbs. I played with *Star Wars* action figures, watched Bugs Bunny cartoons, and ate Frosted Flakes. Yet when Bruce Springsteen's hit song "Born in the U.S.A." reverberated across the airwaves in the eighties, my heart sank.

The song was about the difficulties of life in the U.S. and I saw it as another reminder that I wasn't truly American since I wasn't born here. It created a rift in my psyche that gnawed at my sense of identity. I'm not as American as my Black friends. I'm definitely not as American as my white peers. This sense of patriotic alienation even extended to my Asian friends, as the majority of them could at least claim U.S. citizenship, as they were born in the country. Yet because I was born in Hong Kong and was an immigrant, I saw myself as a second-class citizen. The shame was noted on our formal identification cards. U.S. citizens have passports. As immigrants we had what was known as "green cards" or resident alien cards, which I looked at with disgust. Why did the card have to label me an "alien"? I hated whenever we had to travel and show our proof of residency. In later years, the naming of this card was changed to permanent resident card, but by then the damage was done and, once again, I saw myself as not being truly American.

# Rich Kids Eat at McDonald's

The shame and alienation of being poor added to my sense of separateness even from those around me. Nearly 80 percent of the students at my school qualified for free or reduced-fee lunch. By the time I got to high school, the shame of being poor was unbearable, as I saw the "rich" kids going to lunch at McDonald's or Jack in the Box. I was so ashamed of our socioeconomic background that I gave away my free-lunch card to a friend's older brother. I preferred to buy lunch rather than get it free to distance myself from this daily reminder of my family's financial circumstances.

You would think since so many of the people around us qualified for free lunch, we were all in the same boat, but it wasn't the case. While most of us qualified for free lunch, I felt my family was worse off. The house my parents bought was not only the smallest on the block, it was the smallest among all of my friends's homes. The one-story house had two bedrooms and one bathroom and was approximately 500 square feet. We had no privacy, as my brothers and I slept in the same room. Our house was so small friends wouldn't want to come over to play with us. Even playing outdoors highlighted our poverty.

One of our favorite pastimes was riding our bikes through the neighborhood. The problem was our parents could afford only one bike for the three of us. When we went anywhere with our friends, my middle brother, who was the strongest, would give me a ride for a portion of the way and drop me off. I would then run the remainder of the distance to wherever the kids were biking, while my middle brother went back to pick up our youngest brother and meet us at our final destination. No one ever asked why we didn't have our own bikes, but obviously it wasn't by choice.

A final indelible memory of how poor I felt was when we had bath time. As toddlers my brothers and I took baths together to save money on the hot-water bill. But when we got older and could no longer fit in the tub together, our parents decided we would share the collective bathwater. The order of who was to bathe first was based on seniority. Because I was the oldest, I got the clean, warm water; the middle brother bathed after me; and the youngest was left with the cesspool of cold, brownish bathwater. The sight of the dirty water being recycled for baths made me feel inferior, as I asked other friends if this was common practice. They looked at me with shock.

I also had sibling shame and sought to distance myself from my younger brothers. I had enough struggles fitting in and being accepted as American, so I found ways to create my own sense of identity without having to fear getting rejected along with my brothers.

I joined an Asian basketball league in elementary school and didn't think of asking them to come along and play for their respective age groups. By middle school, I joined after-school clubs and other activities to make friends, but also to create more of a gap between me and my brothers. I don't even recall acknowledging them in the hallways between classes while in middle school.

When we were all in high school, I was invited to attend an Asian-American Christian youth group at a church a couple of miles from our house. Once again, I never considered inviting my brothers, even when friends urged me to do so. I would make up excuses, saying they didn't care about religion, but the truth was I was fearful that if my friends met my brothers they wouldn't like them, they'd reject them, and I'd eventually get rejected as well.

Years later, the pain of my actions pierced me when praying with an African-American pastor who empathized with how the impact of racism and the desire to fit into society led to my actions. She prayed that I would forgive myself, knowing that my actions, while intentional, were not malicious but done out of a fear for self-preservation, identity, and acceptance.

## 'You Can't Get Hurt!'

Both my parents worked in Chinese restaurants and didn't have health or dental insurance. This fact was never told to us directly, but from as young as I can remember, our parents would tell us, "You can't get hurt!" When we played we were mindful that our parents would get extremely upset if we got injured. But children will get hurt; that's a part of life. I recall dribbling a basketball on gravel and slipping and the rocks caused a huge cut on my right thigh. I cried knowing this was a serious injury, but that I wasn't allowed to tell my parents about it. Instead of going home, I walked to my grandmother's house, where she tended to my wounds. I was around eight years old and I recall my grandmother being very upset that I was afraid to go home. She called my mother (her daughter-in-law) and let her know that it was not right that I was scared to go home due to getting injured.

On another occasion, my brother dove into a shallow part of a lake on a hot, summer day. He hit his head on a rock and I gave him my T-shirt to staunch the large gash on his head. I remember him turning to me and our youngest brother, pleading that we not tell our parents. I told him, "Ken, I don't think that's a good idea, but if you really want us to keep it a secret, I'll honor our code as brothers." The secret held up until the middle of the night, when my dad shouted in terror, "What happened to Ken? Why is there blood gushing from his head?" That's when I spilled the beans and told them what happened earlier in the day. My brother was immediately taken to the ER and, eight stitches later, he was patched up, but not before our parents gave us a tongue-lashing for not informing them of the accident. I guess if it was life-threatening, our parents wanted us to tell them about injuries, but short of dying we were to figure it out ourselves. From a psychological perspective, what I learned as a child was that it wasn't okay to get hurt and, if you did get hurt, you had to keep it to yourself.

## Bowl Cuts, Bell-bottoms, and Parachute Pants

To save money, our parents cut our hair rather than take us to a barbershop or salon. Unfortunately, we had the stereotypical Asian bowl cut. It was a traumatic experience, as we would all cry whenever our hair was cut in this manner. In the military, your head is shaved so you will lose your sense of individuality. The same could be said when we got our hair cut. Not only did we get the same bowl cut, we swapped and wore the same shirts and pants, and we were Chinese. The undiscerning eye saw three Chinese kids who looked interchangeable at school and in public.

The anguish of wanting to be myself, separate from my brothers, was palpable, but wearing the same clothes and having the same haircut made many of our classmates clump us together. "There goes the Louie brothers," they would say, as it was too much work for them to differentiate us. When our father saw our distress he tried to reassure us that our hair would grow back faster if we stuck our head out the car windows and let the wind run through it. Sure enough, whenever we got our hair cut you would see three heads popping out of the car windows, regardless of the weather, in hopes that our hair would grow back and help restore our sense of individuality.

By middle school, being self-conscious of my ethnicity, physical appearance, clothes, and socioeconomic status took a firm grip on me. I could no longer endure the teasing. I can still recall overhearing a female student pointing at me and wondering, "Doesn't that guy have another shirt?"

My pant situation wasn't much better. I was wearing out-of-style bell-bottom pants in the seventh grade. I didn't think anything of it until a girl I had a crush on laughed when she saw them and said, "Sam, are those bell-bottoms?" I felt shame and humiliation and vowed never to wear those pants again. But a week later, all the sweatpants I usually wore to school were in the hamper and the only clean pair of pants left were the dreaded bell-bottoms. I was faced with a conundrum: wear the pants and risk exposing myself to more shame or stay home from school and lose an award for perfect attendance, which I was on pace for. This was an excruciating decision, as I was so proud of my perfect attendance from kindergarten up until that point. Still, the potential sting of embarrassment was too much, so I stayed home despite my mom's anger and her own shaming of me for "caring too much about what others think."

A few days later, while playing at my grandparents's home, I came across a stash of what looked like parachute pants. I asked if I could have them, and my grandfather seemed amused and told me to take what I wanted. Parachute pants were all the rage, with hip-hop and breakdancing becoming popular. Only the "rich" kids could afford them, so I thought I had stumbled on fashion gold.

When I tried them on one day before school, there was an intolerable itchy feeling. My mom said it was because the pants were made of wool. Itch or not, I was going to wear them so all could see I was "too legit to quit," to borrow a lyric from the popular rap song by MC Hammer.

I walked confidently into my first-period woodshop class that morning wearing my parachute pants. I scratched my leg a few times because of the annoying wool, but that's a small price to pay for social acceptance. A white, rich kid known as the school fashionista made a beeline toward me, gawked at my pants, and then in a loud, condescending tone said, "Are those supposed to be parachute pants?" I faintly nodded, but the jig was up before it had even started.

## White Families Have Microwaves!

If you're wondering how there could be affluent kids at my school, it's because we were part of a desegregation policy known as "The Seattle Plan" that began in 1972 and lasted nearly three decades. During this period, the Seattle Public School District instituted a voluntary desegregation program in which students from ethnic neighborhoods were bussed to the white areas of the city and vice-versa, as a means to increase racial diversity.

My brothers and I would wake up extremely early and be at the bus stop by six a.m. and take the hour-long ride to West Seattle. I can still recall standing in wet, foggy, cold weather during many fall and winter seasons. This program was a bold move on the part of the school district, and it was met with opposition by many white families. This was reflected in the almost immediate plummeting of white-student enrollment, as those families left for the suburbs or private schools. The policy ended in 1999 due to too much public backlash from both white and black families. As if it wasn't hard enough being poor among my Black and Asian peers, desegregation opened my eyes to a new level of poverty shame, as my white peers not only had nice clothes but lived in houses with microwaves, air-conditioning (considered a luxury in Seattle), and swimming pools.

Former *Seattle Times* photographer John Lok shared his appreciation of his Seattle Plan experience in an interview with the newspaper published on July 29, 2019. In the article Lok expressed how he wants his own children to have similar relationships across cultures and socioeconomic backgrounds. He said, "It's important for them to meet and hear the stories of people who are not like them. People come from all over the globe, and they bring with them different stories, different struggles, different opinions."

In the same vein, I'm truly grateful to have been a part of this program. I met suburban white friends from middle- and upper-middle-class socioeconomic backgrounds, which gave me a better appreciation of the racial and financial disparities between the various neighborhoods. I also glimpsed for the first time that neighborhoods could be safe and people could own dogs as pets as opposed to guard dogs. Seeing affluence, or at least middle-class living, inspired me to look for ways to make my own money, instead of relying on birthdays or holidays for an occasional dollar.

# Working Hard for the Money

My awareness of how our family lacked money for toys, clothes, and treats like candy or ice cream was criticized by my parents and relatives. They saw my complaints as a lack of gratitude. To further this point, Mom would share how our father was so impoverished growing up that the only toy he had was one small ball. Our uncles added to this with their own stories of catching dragonflies and tying strings on their tails as a creative means to make their own version of kites. I didn't care too much for these Hong Kong scenarios of poverty, as I couldn't relate. I was in America and wanted what the other kids had: bikes, Legos, and an allowance so I could buy things. We never got an allowance, so the only money came from birthdays, Christmas, Chinese New Year, or when our mom went shopping at the mall.

While at the mall, she would give us each a dollar to hang out at the arcade. The cost to play a video game or pinball machine was a quarter, so we had enough money to play four games. We had to think of ways to stretch our dollar, knowing our mom could be gone for up to two hours.

At home, we never had soft drinks, candy, or snacks like potato chips or cookies. We drank tap water and occasionally had apple or orange juice. We also never had desserts, unless apples and oranges count. With just the bare necessities at home when it came to food, clothing, and entertainment, my mind was preoccupied with ways to make money once I got older.

In middle school, some of my friends had paper routes and I wanted to join them to earn money. This desire intensified after the parachute-pants and bell-bottoms debacles. A friend must've sensed my desperation, and he asked if I wanted to help him on his weekly route. I knew my mom would be against it, so I lied and told her student government was now twice a week after school. After a couple of weeks my mother knew I was lying, and once she knew the truth she called my friend's family (they were also Chinese) and told them I wasn't allowed to work. I sulked and was furious at this unilateral decision.

Undeterred, one year later, I jumped at another opportunity to help a friend deliver the *Seattle Times* every day. My mom objected, but I didn't care anymore. I refused to listen to her and started making money for the first time in my life. It felt like true financial independence, as I made more than $100 per month. I could buy whatever I wanted, play video games, and eat junk food at my discretion. I eventually took over an adjacent paper route and had the responsibility of sixty daily subscriptions, which was one of the largest routes in the neighborhood and took up to two hours each day. It taught me a lot about responsibility, as I had to deliver the newspaper in the afternoon each day after school and early in the morning on weekends. I was also responsible for collecting money. At the end of the month, I would go door-to-door to collect the monthly fees, which took significant time, as many owners weren't home or they'd ask me to come back later because they didn't have the eight dollars (the cost of a daily subscription). After delivering newspapers for nearly two years, I turned sixteen and was legally able to get a real job.

## Not Black Enough or White Enough

I was so excited to be interviewing for my first real job when I was sixteen year old. My only reservation was the demographics of the employees, as everyone working at this McDonald's was Black. How would they view me? Would being Asian impact my hiring? Nah, why would they care? I thought to myself. Since I was the first in my family to apply for a job that required an interview (my uncles and other relatives got jobs in Chinese restaurants through friends), I wasn't sure how to prepare for an official job interview. What would they ask me? Do I need to lie and tell them my allegiance to fast food was limited to McDonald's? Should I mention I have a fondness for Colonel Sander's Kentucky Fried Chicken? I didn't have anyone to role-play with or to help me with these questions, but I had learned that interviews required me to dress my best and leave a positive impression. I put on my Sunday best: the sweater I used in my yearbook picture, black slacks, and dress shoes. I was ready to take Ronald McDonald by storm.

The tall, Black manager introduced himself and we sat down at one of the tables and he asked me a few questions. Coming from a Chinese culture, where we respect authority figures such as a potential boss, I made sure to show respect by nodding a lot and limiting what I said to him. In other words, even if he asked me a question, I was taught to stay silent or to say as little as possible. There's a quote by the Chinese philosopher Lao Tzu: "Those who know do not speak. Those who speak do not know." This saying probably led to some major cultural confusion that day, with the manager wondering how he could hire me if I was so quiet or reserved. I didn't get the job, and I don't know the exact reason for not getting hired, but I'm sure my perceived shyness didn't help. Years later, this experience came up when I was a participant in a men's group therapy. Unbeknownst to me, there was a lot of repressed pain from the experience, as I inexplicably burst into tears while describing it. The pain of wanting this job but getting rejected possibly because I wasn't "Black enough" finally hit me. I'm not saying the manager was racist or had ill-intent, but back then Asians were very new to South Seattle and thus had limited trust or rapport with the Black community. Despite the setback, I was still determined to get a job somewhere.

The next job I applied for was at a car wash in a white neighborhood in a city bordering South Seattle. The entire staff was white, which definitely felt awkward. Regardless, I wanted to work and make some real cash and saw this as a great opportunity compared to my paper route (where $3.25 was the hourly wage). When I applied, the manager asked me to complete a psychological test. I didn't think much of it, but shortly after I started the test, I could feel the sweat dripping down my forehead and in my armpits. The questions looked innocent enough, but caused a lot of consternation: "Have you ever told a lie?" "Have you ever taken anything that wasn't yours?" "Do you ever get angry?" "Do you ever have problems?" I answered "no" to all these and similar questions, as I didn't want it to reflect poorly on me. I wanted to portray the positive image of a hard-working, honest immigrant. I didn't get hired there either and wondered if the test was rigged against people like me or if it was because I wasn't "white enough."

I was discouraged, as it began to feel like race was getting in the way. Ironically, when my uncle heard I was looking for a job, he placed a phone call to a friend who was a manager at a Chinese grocery store, who hired me on the spot without an interview. I was a grocery bagger, but it was a lot more arduous than the baggers at stores like Kroger, Albertsons, or Safeway. Beyond bagging groceries and stocking the shelves with canned Asian goods, we also had to sort, load, and unload 100-pound bags of rice that came in weekly. I was a scrawny teenager and barely weighed more than the rice I was lifting. I had a co-worker who was much bigger and stronger and I would dread it whenever he said, "Hey, Sam. It's time to do the rice!" That was my warning to prepare to sweat, as we'd spend an hour lifting and organizing the rice in the warehouse. The warehouse was cavernous with nearly a dozen different varieties of rice stacked thirty feet high from floor to ceiling. When the main store was low on rice, it was our job to clamber up the various piles, find the rice that was needed, put them on our shoulders, and walk them to the main store two blocks away and unload them. It was hard, physical labor, but at least I was earning my keep.

The cashiers at the store were all immigrant, Chinese women. When I was bagging groceries, they would gently poke fun at my broken Chinese; I spoke a hybrid of Cantonese punctuated with English. So even at a Chinese grocery store, I still wasn't "Chinese enough."

## *Leave It to Beaver* on Television

My family's first television set was black and white. It had three channels and you had to physically get up and turn the knob if you wanted to change the channels, as remote controls were not invented yet. Mom watched it both for entertainment after her own long day at work as a waitress, but it was also her means of learning English. Mom enjoyed TV. She would laugh, smile, and try to pronounce words she heard. She gravitated toward sit-coms. I vividly remember not only the shows she watched—*Leave It to Beaver, Hogan's Heroes, Bewitched, WKRP in Cincinnati, Laverne & Shirley*—but the accompanying theme songs.

Eventually, I figured out that TV shows weren't random but could be predictable if one knew how to read the TV guide in newspapers or magazines. This felt like a godsend. I was enamored with what TV could do to me. It transported me to another world, where I could escape the fear of crime and trying to navigate this country on my own. I was the first in my family and extended family to go to school in the U.S. I was trailblazing both for myself and the entire Louie family; my grandparents, parents, uncles, and aunts had never gone through the U.S. educational system from kindergarten to college and into a mainstream American workplace. I was the tip of the spear and no one would be able to relate to my new experiences. Each transition, juncture, or challenge would need to be tackled on my own. The expectations were high and, with nowhere to go with the fears and anxiety, I looked for ways to numb out. Television was one of my earliest ways to do so.

My needs for nurturing, comfort, support, and validation came through the shows. Masculinity was shaped by watching *Magnum, P.I., Buck Rogers in the 25th Century, Battlestar Galactica, CHiPs*, and *The A-Team*. I found what family could look like in *The Brady Bunch*. The parents portrayed such love and tenderness to their children, even when there were disagreements and challenges. There were hugs, kisses, and compliments. Even in admonishment, there was love. I wanted that for my family, but knew our Chinese culture of emotional stoicism wasn't going to provide it for me, so watching it on TV was my substitute.

During the summers I discovered soap operas such as *The Young and the Restless*, *As the World Turns*, and *Days of Our Lives*. These soaps had me transfixed like never before. I saw love, or what I thought was love, being demonstrated in the form of romance. When the actors kissed, I viewed this as the most intimate act of human connection. Is this what was needed for me to be close to another human being? I was only ten years old when the connection between romance and sex as the ultimate expression of closeness was formed in my mind. I was too young, shy, and poor to feel a girl would like me, so I never entertained the thought of kissing a real girl. Nudity wasn't as accessible as it is today, but some friends had cable TV where pornographic movies were "scrambled" (i.e. a form of encryption to control access to paid content). While we couldn't see anything, we could hear the moans and groans.

## It Looks Like an Anteater

If hating myself for my culture wasn't bad enough, I began hating my penis because it looked like an anteater. In Hong Kong and many parts of the world, children do not get circumcised. But circumcision is common in the U.S. The dissonance was most readily apparent when Mom took us to swimming lessons. She asked if my brothers and I would prefer to take showers at the swimming pool after the lessons, and all three of us vehemently said no. The showers did not have dividers, so we would be naked in plain view of other kids. I could not bear having our peers ridiculing us for our uncircumcised penises; we endured staying in our wet and cold swim trunks until we got home to take private showers.

In middle school, I learned that in the PE classes, boys and girls had to take showers. I was horrified. How was I to keep my circumcision secret from others? To make matters worse, the dry towels were guarded by the PE teacher, and you could get one only by walking from the showers to him, where he'd inspect each boy to ensure we were thoroughly washed. Fortunately, I saw another Asian boy cup his genital area with his hand, so that's what I did for those two years of middle school.

Beyond having a penis that looked like an anteater, I also became worried about the health repercussions of being uncircumcised. When I was in high school, a radio station had sex as one of the topics and was taking listener questions. I called and was live on the air asking the doctor if I needed to get circumcised because of my health concerns. He responded that health isn't a concern so long as I washed it regularly. Still, it came down to acceptance and I couldn't bear it much longer. By the time I was eighteen, I had saved up enough money (about $2,000) to get circumcised. I made an appointment at the local hospital and had the surgery. I didn't tell my parents or any of my friends, except a mentor from church who I confided in, as someone had to drive me home from the hospital. It wasn't instantaneous, but over time I became more comfortable taking public showers.

Boys that go through childhood without any frank conversations about sex are vulnerable to feeling inadequate about their sense of masculinity. Nowhere is that more evident than in relationship to penis size. Being uncircumcised was shameful enough; now I have to wonder about the adequacy or inadequacy of my private parts. Since sexual jokes and references highlight the desirability of size, this was a growing concern for me. Was I big enough? One older kid in the neighborhood gave me a couple of porn magazines and told me if I masturbated enough, eventually my penis would get bigger. I was naïve and believed him, and eager to put this to the test.

## All My Dreams in a Department Store Catalog

Before I became fixated on romantic or sexual material, I was still exhibiting obsessive and compulsive behaviors. My parents would get department-store catalogs from places like Sears or JCPenney. These catalogs were thick with hundreds of items for a shopper to peruse. They would display pictures of items being sold, along with their descriptions and the corresponding price. I pored over the sections related to toys, electronics, and sporting-goods equipment. I would circle and highlight or cut out the things I wanted. All my dreams of what I wanted in life then were found in these department-store catalogs. It was soothing to go into a trance-like state and just imagine what life would be like if I had the object of my desire.

Eventually, the lingerie ads caught my attention and I would dream of being with the women featured in the ads. Because of my insecurities with my ethnic background, I intentionally focused on the white women. If I was with them, would they love me? Would they find me worthwhile or attractive? Would they accept me? Even before puberty, many nights were spent just looking at the women and touching myself. It felt good to be able to take care of myself emotionally through this simple act of masturbation. All my fears and worries would disappear when I went into fantasyland. Lingerie ads soon gave way to real-life celebrities that I became infatuated with on television and in the movies.

## Wonder Woman Was White

Cinderella was white. Princess Leia was white. Charlie's Angels were white. Wonder Woman was white. Everywhere I turned, the standard of beauty in this country looked white. The male heroes were also white. Tom Selleck in *Magnum, P.I.* David Hasselhoff of *Knight Rider*. Luke Skywalker and Han Solo. The sitcoms my brothers and I watched with our mom were also noticeably white, so it makes sense that I viewed relationships and the desire for romance through this same prism.

I can still remember several on-screen women I was attracted to: Erin Gray from *Buck Rogers in the 25th Century* and *Silver Spoons*, Kelly LeBrock from *Weird Science*, and Kristian Alfonso, who played Hope on the NBC soap opera *Days of Our Lives*. With no expressive love at home, I associated their on-screen personalities of care and concern as surrogate maternal figures who I could project my insecurities toward. In my head, they in return listened to me and loved me, regardless of my life circumstances, especially in moments punctuated by abandonment.

## Fear Is My First Memory

My first distinct memory is one of fear. I was stuck on a merry-go-round as my mother was walking away trying to persuade me to get off and follow her. I was paralyzed with fear while I watched her fading into the distance. The sight left me in a state of panic. I came to see her as unsafe.

The impact of this sense of abandonment became evident when I hurt myself when I was eight years old trying to dribble the basketball on gravel. In therapy as an adult, I processed how I internalized that my mom would be displeased with my injury. I wrote this journal entry following that session in June 2003:

> *I cried so hard in therapy my eyes still hurt (11 hours later). We touched on some very raw feelings today regarding my perception of myself. I have learned in the past that I could never hurt physically and ever since then it translated into trying to never get hurt emotionally.*
>
> *I get so scared of being rejected and not accepted by others that it's hard for me to allow others to see that I'm vulnerable as opposed to being all-knowing. I don't ever want someone to think I'm inadequate or uninformed so I've done a lot of hiding.*

Another core wounding occurred on a summer afternoon when I was ten years old. Having fun in a low-income neighborhood meant using your imagination. During those long days, with no money or organized activities, we would meet other kids in the neighborhood and use our creativity to play. Sometimes we caught bees in mason jars, other times we made mud balls in my grandmother's backyard.

One day, some kids in our community decided to take abandoned car tires, walk them up a hill, and roll them down as a form of competition to see which tire could go the farthest. As the other tires rolled to a stop, to my astonishment mine kept going. I was going to win! Not only did my tire go the farthest, it went so far that the only reason it stopped was because it hit a parked car. All the other kids quickly scattered. I not only stayed but walked down to the house where it was parked and told the owner what had happened. He asked if I lived close by and I walked him to my home.

When we arrived, my mom answered the door and the man told her she would have to pay for the damages to his car. My mom, in an attempt to avoid paying, told him in halting, broken English, "Me no money! Take him! Take him!" When she uttered this, she was pushing me out the door in his direction. Panic pierced my soul. I remember kicking, crying, and screaming. The guy got spooked and left. I walked back into our house like a dog with his tail between his legs. I was shocked, hurt, confused, and inconsolable. My mother, though, was relieved. She offered no words of comfort, so I harbored this traumatizing experience internally. This incident left an indelible scar of abandonment on my soul. I never wanted to experience that again.

This fear of abandonment would unconsciously impact how I viewed relationships moving forward. My juvenile mind interpreted this event as one of maternal rejection. To close the gap, I sought ways to get closer to my mother without her knowledge. When she was busy, I would go into her lingerie drawer and smell her underwear or pantyhose. She would wash our clothes in the bathtub and, when she wore loose clothing, I could see her breasts. It was the first time I had seen nudity of any kind in the flesh and it was both exhilarating and shameful. I was disgusted at the arousal, but also fascinated. Despite the shame, whenever my mother washed clothes, I made it a point to get a glimpse. Beyond the fear and fascination, I truly viewed it as my one opportunity to connect with her.

## Who Is My Father?

My dad was also distant. He worked long hours in the kitchen to support the family, and when he was home he had no time to invest in us. He could not speak English and I couldn't speak Chinese well enough to communicate with him. In addition, there was a significant cultural divide. What could my dad possibly understand about growing up in America since he was raised in Hong Kong? How could we connect emotionally?

The few positive memories I have of bonding with my father are from Sundays (his one day off), when he'd ask me and my brothers to massage him by gently tapping our fists on the back of his neck, down his back, and down the back of his legs and calves. It lasted no more than ten or twenty minutes, but it was the closest I felt to him.

I never knew my father on an intimate level and that hurts. I knew him only from his activities: his work as a chef, his downtime watching Chinese soap operas, or playing mahjong with relatives. What motivated him? What inspired him? What fears or concerns did he have? None of this was revealed to me. The hurt is compounded, as he never knew me. My dreams, longings, concerns, and fears could not be shared with him. It's a tremendous relational loss few men are willing to acknowledge, lest they appear weak. Culturally, it's also viewed as shaming your parents to verbalize being disappointed in them. Having never received my father's blessing or approval, my deep yearning for validation made me ripe for codependency and people-pleasing, even if that meant being bullied by others.

## Friends, How Many of Us Have Them?

By the end of elementary school, I felt I was fairly well integrated into the African-American neighborhood and was comfortable being a minority within a minority. I belonged to a local track and field team on which I was the only non-Black member. I wasn't a good runner, but since a couple of my friends from school were on the team, I decided to join them as a means to pass the time.

After school, we would walk a mile to the community center, where we would practice at the outdoor track. One day my two Black friends took me behind a mini-mart and punched me in the gut numerous times. I was stunned because I had not done anything to provoke the attack. They stopped when they saw a police car pull into the mini-mart. As the officer got out and started walking into the store, he noticed tears streaming down my face and asked, "Hey, son. Are you OK?" I nodded that I was fine, even though I was not. My friends didn't hit me any more after that, but they didn't apologize either. The only words spoken by them were, "Sam, you're lucky you didn't say anything." That veiled threat became a mantra for life: "Don't say anything." Don't tell others when you've been hurt, sad, scared, angry, or anything of significance. It was another reminder that I needed to stay silent. I also learned that you can't truly trust your friends, since you never know when they might turn on you for no reason.

In sixth grade, I had a white friend who sat next to me in the classroom. I considered him a friend because we had known each other for the past two years and played at recess together. He never did anything malicious until that year. Like clockwork, during our quiet reading time after lunch, I would invariably get a painful whack against the back of my neck. I never said anything to him or the teacher. I had learned to keep the peace as a means to garner acceptance in America. Needless to say, I felt betrayed, hurt, and confused by why my friends would turn on me. In all these instances I wondered why I was teased. Was it because I was different? Was it because I was Asian?

With no one to talk to about these incidents, it was easy to escape through TV, video games, sports, or sexual fantasy through my stash of department-store catalogs.

## Can I Marry My Teacher?

In middle school, I began having crushes on some of my female teachers. One who I still remember fondly is Ms. Mars. I seriously thought she was sent from heaven. She taught math and was kind, loving, and encouraging. I fantasized about marrying her. These positive and affirming feminine interactions were new to me and I craved more of them. Given the opportunity, I would try to sit near the teachers I had crushes on. I would arrive to class early and be the last to leave after the bell rang, extracting as much time as possible in their presence.

I was also exposed to the ritual of scanning for girls in the annual yearbook. It was a personal treasure trove of visual stimuli and fantasy. I still had the lingerie models in the department-store catalogs at my disposal, but the yearbook was personal, as I felt more of a connection with girls my age. In the store catalogs the fantasy was removed from reality, whereas the cute girls in the yearbook were part of my daily reality. In other words, I had the opportunity to see the girls I liked at school. I spent endless hours just gazing at the pictures of the girls, while thinking that life could be so carefree, fun, and meaningful if I was in a relationship with one of them.

When I entered high school, I was tiring of just hoping, wishing, and looking at yearbook pictures, lingerie ads, and soap-opera actresses. I wanted a real relationship. In the ninth grade, I started attending an Asian church's youth group in our neighborhood. There were boys and girls from other schools in the area who attended the youth group and I couldn't have been happier. I thought it was better than isolating myself at home, so I went regularly.

By the end of the first year, I liked a girl who was a junior at a different high school and I flirted with her. Shockingly she liked me, too. We didn't do much, as it was more of a "puppy love" relationship, where I went to her house a few times to watch music videos. But she was the first girl I held hands with and that moment is still frozen in time. It felt like a jolt of electricity ran through my body as I held and caressed the softness of a feminine hand, leading instantly to arousal. The relationship fizzled out due to my own insecurities. Her family lived in a nice part of Seattle and was financially secure, and when I saw her home I compared it with my own and felt she would never want to be with me, so I just stopped talking to her and made up some excuse of needing to focus on basketball or school.

## Basketball, Atari, and Michael Jackson

Other means to self-medicate my feelings were through basketball, video games, and music. Basketball was an activity that I picked up in elementary school and realized it was an accessible sport that could make me feel good. All I needed was a ball and a hoop. I could play by myself or with others. Many days, to escape the drudgery of disconnection at home, I went to the school playground, regardless of the weather, to shoot baskets by myself.

Because it was Seattle, many of those days were in the rain or cold. The weather wasn't a deterrent because I was getting a high of sorts whenever the ball went through the hoop. It was addictive. It was healthy at first, but later I learned it was just another means for me to self-medicate any negative feelings I had about myself or what I perceived the world thought about me.

If I wasn't playing basketball outdoors, I was playing video games indoors. My first taste of video games was through an Atari 2600 home console on which we'd play games like *Space Invaders*, *Frogger*, and *Pac-Man*. In the years to come, I would gravitate toward video games at the arcade and mini-mart, which became a weekend and summer escape. Since we didn't have a lot of money,

I wasn't going to spend money willy-nilly. I would go and watch the other kids to learn patterns, so when I felt confident to play I could maximize my quarter. I also read video-game magazines and memorized strategies and patterns for games like *Super Mario Brothers*. I got good enough where I could play one quarter for up to two hours on *Super Mario Brothers*, proud I could save the princess by advancing through all the levels.

I also played pinball. In pinball there were opportunities to win a free game if you got a high enough score or had a "match" (i.e. at the end of a game, the system randomly selects two digits and if they match the last two of your score you win a game).

Michael Jackson was very popular and I had bootlegged copies of his album *Thriller*. As cassette tapes gave way to CDs, my father bought me a CD player for my birthday. In a short amount of time, I had amassed nearly 200 R & B, hip-hop, and rap albums. Some of favorite artists included Atlantic Starr, Babyface, New Edition, and LL Cool J. I would isolate myself for hours just listening to music, as another means to disconnect from my family.

As I entered puberty, my obsession with basketball, video games, and music gave way to romantic intrigue and sexual fantasy.

## Ms. Pac-Man Teaches Me the Birds and the Bees

As you can probably imagine, my parents didn't educate me on the birds and the bees. I played one of the Pac-Man games, where a stork would deliver a baby Pac-Man, and that was how I thought babies came into the world. No one told me it involved our genitals until middle school, when my brothers and I were talking to our uncle and he told us, "You stick your penis in a woman and that's how babies get made." I was disgusted, nauseated, and confounded. It didn't make any sense to me and I refused to believe it until puberty.

Puberty was marked by the growth of facial and pubic hair. I also was getting frequent erections watching kissing scenes in movies and on television. It finally dawned on me that my uncle was probably right. Because I was so naïve, I didn't know what it meant to masturbate. Friends would joke about it, but I didn't know how to do it, so masturbation didn't take hold until college.

When I was seventeen, I was dating another girl from our Asian-American church youth group. Once it got physical, it seemed that's all I could focus on. One day when her parents and siblings were out of the house we had sex for the first time. I didn't know what to make of it, as I had never had a wet dream or masturbated prior to this and the sensation of ejaculating caught me off guard. I was embarrassed because I thought I couldn't control my bladder and was urinating. In addition, because we were both going to church, there was immense shame of having committed an unpardonable sin.

This first sexual experience, while shameful, also opened a new world to me. While basketball, television, video games, and department-store catalogs were great means of numbing out, this felt like the solution. Sex and sexual stimulation felt like they fit perfectly for my needs, like a key to a lock. I felt safe, wanted, loved, and free of worry from all external issues. In other words, I was hooked.

## A Low SAT Score

I was accepted into the University of Washington because of the school's affirmative-action policies aimed at ethnic diversity. I know it wasn't because of my SAT score; I scored 800 out of a possible 1600. I took the test twice to make sure it wasn't a typo. This was humiliating because I heard from friends you could get a 700 just by signing your name on the test. I had a friend who scored nearly 800 points on the math section alone. This obviously made me even more self-conscious. Years later, a Korean friend told me he scored 1500 on his SAT. When I gushed at his achievement he downplayed it and responded, "Sam, my parents put me in annual summer SAT prep classes for five years starting in middle school! If you went through the same classes, you would've done well, too." Maybe, but that wasn't my reality.

My reality was I was the first person in my lineage to go to college. The expectations compounded because my brothers decided not to attend college. (One attended community college for a year and the other decided to work full time as a bank teller.) I had no idea what to do with my life. My extended relatives were all working in blue-collar, immigrant jobs. My mom suggested the stereotypical professions of doctor, engineer, or businessman. I didn't know what I was good at, but I knew I sucked at math and science, so those careers were out of the question.

One area that piqued my interest, ever since my days of delivering the newspaper, was journalism. I had always wondered how those stories got in the paper and thought it would be an exciting career. My mother religiously watched the local news, so I thought this could be a career she'd support. But I never told her I was planning to major in journalism until I was officially accepted into the university. When I received the acceptance letter in the mail, I immediately told her, thinking she'd share in my excitement. Instead, she told me she was vehemently against this idea, citing the lack of Asian men in news. I agreed to switch careers and she proposed I go into teaching, as that is a well-respected profession in Asia. Not only did I switch my major to education, I transferred to a university ninety miles north of Seattle known for its education department.

This was a true college experience. I was no longer a commuter student, but living on campus. The school was also much smaller than the University of Washington and I enjoyed bonding with other students in the dorms and, later, in an apartment off-campus.

Being away from home was a blessing and a curse. I was able to structure my time and study as required to get decent grades. But the lack of attachment to my close friends and family from home led me to seeking love in romantic relationships. From the moment I arrived on campus, I was hoping romance would fill the void in my heart. Yet due to my own insecurities about my attractiveness as an Asian male, I felt limited. I was told by other dorm-mates there were girls who liked me, but I dismissed them, thinking there was no way a white girl would like me.

Due to my own internal oppression, I viewed white women as the top of the pyramid in terms of attractiveness. While I found Asian women attractive, they were seen as backups and not my priority. If anything, I felt dating an Asian woman would be too easy, since we already shared the same background. There were girls in my classes that I wanted to ask out, but I was too shy to do so. The fear of rejection was too strong. Instead, I resorted to going out and meeting women in bars. That felt safer because everyone was drinking and I didn't have to do as much talking. In other words, I could let my body do the talking for me by flirting, dancing, or kissing. Learning how to read body cues became my way to gauge if a woman was interested. This was preferred; there were no words of rejection to deal with. In what seemed like a blur, I had a handful of casual sex partners—I'd get drunk, have sex, and then continue the sexual encounters for a short time, before moving on to another woman. In one memorable early encounter, I was kissing a woman and liked her enough to ask if this meant we were a couple. She responded, "No, we're just making out!" That was hard to hear and it steeled my belief that relationships weren't desired of me, so the hunt to keep things solely sexual continued.

I was depressed and felt intense shame during these sexual encounters. I never cared about my health, so I didn't wear protection. If anything, I was hoping I'd catch AIDS and die, which would validate my feelings of worthlessness and defectiveness. I was torn over my sexual behaviors. I yearned for a relationship, but had no idea how to get it. I had been preconditioned by American media and machismo into believing that bedding as many women as possible was my ticket to masculinity. This became my pursuit in college, regardless of who I hurt.

One woman who liked my public persona as a nice, outgoing guy expressed interest in me. But after it became sexual, I grew cold, distant, and mean. I wanted nothing more to do with her after we had sex. I still remember her crying when she left my apartment. I felt terrible for having hurt her, but realized the fear of being in a relationship was too intense, no matter how sweet and nice the women were.

## I Can't Get Hard

The college I attended was close to Vancouver, British Columbia, where prostitution and gambling are legal. Some friends from Seattle would occasionally pick me up and we'd spend the weekend in Vancouver gambling, eating, and going to clubs. One time, they decided to hire a prostitute to give me oral sex. Since it was free, I thought I'd oblige, but it was a very intimidating experience. The prostitute asked me to put on a condom, but I struggled to get an erection. I was only twenty years old, and the forced nature of this interaction made it extremely uncomfortable for me. She was curt and demeaning, saying, "Are you going to get hard or what?" I tried to muster some arousal; however, the pressure to respond immediately was too much, especially knowing my friends were waiting outside the motel. I eventually left with no erection or orgasm. When my friends asked me about the experience, I lied and told them it was great.

Back on campus, I decided to try to find a real relationship. It was my senior year and I met another student who was a friend of a friend. There was some unspoken rule that I couldn't treat her like I did the other women. So after hooking up, we decided to be officially boyfriend and girlfriend. The relationship lasted about eight months, a miracle on my part. But I don't remember ever asking questions to get to know her. What I do recall is finding ways to enter her home secretly when her parents were asleep, so the two of us could have sex. It was purely a sexual relationship, as my skills at intimacy were limited.

Majoring in education was also difficult, because I had no real desire to be a teacher. I was doing it to placate my mom.

## Asian Shame and Success

In the typical Asian-American household, success is often related to honor and community. Educational attainment and financial success are clear markers of reflecting that honor and prestige back to your parents and family lineage. For children of Asian immigrants, the pressure to succeed can be suffocating. They may be told they must succeed or else their parents's sacrifices and hardships would be all for naught.

Birth order and gender can place an additional burden on the oldest child of immigrants. For the oldest son, he has traditionally carried both the ancestral weight of honor and the weight of shame if he disappoints, fails, or doesn't meet his parental or cultural expectations. As the oldest son of the oldest son, I was to chart the waters of success for my younger brothers and the numerous cousins to follow, especially since I was the first true American in my family. My parents knew success only through the lens of what their friends's children were doing. Teaching was an honorable profession, I kept telling myself when another voice kept whispering to me to be true to my desires and interests.

I had accepted my lot in life and was mindlessly plugging away at becoming a teacher when serendipity intervened in the form of a new friendship when I was one semester shy of graduating. Ironically, at this teaching university, I met a Korean-American who was majoring in journalism and writing stories for the school newspaper. We became fast friends from our shared cultural and professional aspirations. Since he knew I wanted to join the journalism ranks, he suggested I call the local television station. Long story short, I had the gumption to set up an interview with the general manager of the station, who liked me enough that she approved an internship with the news department without even asking the news director for her opinion.

For the rest of my semester, I woke up at four a.m. on weekdays, spent my mornings in the newsroom helping the anchor with her scripts, calling the local police station about possible stories, and other related functions. It wasn't much, but it was what I wanted. I still recall walking with a pep in my step, feeling alive with a sense of purpose that had been lost in my attempt to convince myself and others I wanted to be a teacher.

I was so buoyed with confidence that I elected to drop out of the school of education and graduate with a history degree. My best friend thought I was crazy and asked if I knew what the repercussions were. "Did you tell your parents?" he asked. My heart skipped a beat, as the gravity of defying my cultural norms was now becoming very real.

Not too long after switching majors, I decided to share the news with my parents. They weren't happy, to say the least, but I told them not to worry, as I had lined up another TV internship in Seattle at a station that was highly reputable. My mom watched their newscast regularly, so her posture softened a bit.

## Two Asian Interns

In 1995, I was accepted as an intern at the Seattle NBC station. The station had a popular thirty-minute entertainment show called *Evening Magazine* that covered unique, local feature stories. I was one of two interns selected for the show and both of us coincidentally were Asian. (The other was a Vietnamese-American woman.) I was always conscious of race and being with another Asian intern made me uncomfortable. I was worried how the sight of two Asian interns would look to others in the office. Were we picked because we were Asian? Would the other employees treat us any differently? I was about to get my first lesson in office race relations.

The show was staffed with just a handful of producers and reporters. In other words, you had to see each other. But what was odd was, despite our cheerful disposition, the producers rarely talked or engaged with us interns. There was even a Filipino producer who seemed to give us the coldest of shoulders. It felt like a betrayal. Shouldn't she try to help us or encourage us? Then again, I could see she was trying to maintain workplace neutrality. In other words, if she befriended us, maybe she worried her white peers would see her as giving favoritism based solely on race.

For weeks on end, the producers were indifferent to us. I eventually chalked it up to the possibility of interns being viewed as the lowest tier on the totem pole. But a day came when I saw their faces light up when the prior intern returned to regale them with stories of his current life. This hero's welcome from the producers confirmed my suspicion that race did play a role in who people interacted with in the workplace and how. They obviously felt more of a kinship with a white guy than two Asian-Americans from poor immigrant backgrounds.

The one instance a producer did take interest in me was when she shared that the show was going to do a story on a popular video-game console that was just released. She told me my job was to put the console together. She came in with the box, plopped it on my desk, and, as she was walking away, said something like, "I know you can do it. It's in your blood!" I felt a sense of indignation, as this sort of racial microaggression and stereotype was familiar to me growing up. I thought it would end in adulthood and in a professional workplace. Lesson learned— be on high alert because stupid stuff will come out of people's mouths no matter their level of education or job title. I went into journalism primarily because I'm not tech-savvy or mechanically minded. After stewing on her comment, I thought about just smashing the console, but that would've dishonored not only me but given all Asians a bad name. The only thing left was to preserve my cultural heritage and find a way to put the console together. I spent the next few hours tinkering with it, until it finally worked, much to my pride. The only other thing I had ever put together was my futon in college, and short of graduating that felt like my other biggest accomplishment.

By the time the internship ended, I began applying to smaller stations in Eastern Washington for a reporter position. In one interview with a news director, she asked me why I didn't consider a job in the import/export industry because of my background. I was perplexed because I truly didn't know what it meant at the time, nor did I understand the racial undertones. I brushed the question aside and told her I wanted to be the male version of Connie Chung (the first Asian-American to co-anchor a major network evening news program).

After a few more interviews, I somehow scheduled one with the general manager at the ABC station in Yakima, Washington. The GM asked if I had written any news stories and I replied, "No, but I do have these English papers from college so you can see how I write." I don't know if it was my audacity or naivete, but he glanced at the topics of my papers and read the one titled "Black Standard English." There must have been something I wrote that he connected with. When he was finished, he glanced up at me and shared how he spoke this way growing up in a Black neighborhood in Chicago. Immediately thereafter, he told me I could start next week in the news department. Not only did I get accepted, but it was a paid internship, which was unheard of at the time. Even now, a paid internship in local television news is rare because the position is so coveted that young college graduates will happily work for free in exchange for the experience. Years later, I found out the general manager continued the paid internship to other minorities interested in journalism. I beamed with pride knowing I had left a good enough impression that more opportunities were available to those from similar backgrounds.

My internship consisted of working as what's known in television news as a "one-man-band"; I was the reporter, videographer, and editor. After doing that for six months, I had enough material for a solid résumé reel. I applied for a reporter position in Missoula, Montana, where the station was looking for someone who could shoot, write, and edit his own stories. When I was hired, I was thrilled and worried. Part of it was tied to professional fears, the other was linked to racial anxiety.

## Big Sky Montana

Missoula is a small college town located on the westernmost edge of Montana. It's a beautiful town nestled in a gorgeous valley, just more than 100 miles south of Glacier National Park. The entire western portion of Montana is surrounded by spectacular mountains and wildlife.

Before moving there for work, I had been through Montana only as a child, when my parents drove us to Yellowstone National Park. Beyond the natural wonders, I could also recall how out of place our family looked. Whether at restaurants, motels, or tourist attractions, we stuck out as the only non-whites around.

By the time I was ready to head off for my first full-time position as a news reporter, I wondered aloud if people in Montana would accept me. Acceptance meant myriad things. How would I be treated? Would they like me? Would they view me as a foreigner? Would I be teased, mocked, or, worse, assaulted? Professionally, would my racial background limit who would feel comfortable being interviewed by me? Along with the increased racial anxieties came the escalated cultural fear of failure. That fear loomed larger than the proverbial "Big Sky" of Montana.

In the cold Montana winter of 1995, my parents drove with me to start my career. They spent one night with me at the extended-stay Motel 6. Dad tried to teach me a few dishes to cook and they both gave me some standard Chinese sayings, such as "Remember to listen to your boss!" and "Stay away from bad people!" When they left the next morning, my heart ached and I exploded in tears. It was brief but intense. I had no idea it was connected to my fears and concerns of trying to do right in their eyes and the eyes of our family, who had sacrificed a lot to give me this opportunity in America. But success and life was now up to me to figure out; it felt like the umbilical cord to support was cut for good.

My work as a "one-man band" in Montana was physically exhausting. The equipment was heavy and we had to trudge through snow, wind, and extreme cold, which I was not accustomed to. But I knew what needed to be done so I worked as much as I could. I even volunteered to do the weather forecasts on the weekends as a means to garner more on-camera experience. The hours were long and the pay was embarrassing. My annual salary was $13,998, to be exact. This stuck out to me for a number of reasons. Before having a college degree, I worked as a lifeguard for the city of Seattle and was making nearly twice as much as this. Prior to signing the contract with the station in Montana, I asked my boss if he could throw in two extra dollars so the contract would be listed at an even $14,000. My boss shrugged, looked at me with a wry smile, and responded, "Sam, you know I can't do that." I quickly realized this was not the rich and glamorous profession I had envisioned.

One sidenote about money: Up until this point I had prided myself on being fiscally responsible. I had a credit card, but always paid off the balance each month. But because of my meager salary, I was using my credit card to pay for essentials like gas and groceries and was carrying debt. I winced knowing each transaction was putting me into further debt with an exorbitant interest rate. After a while, I was resigned to the growing debt and became numb to it. I didn't want to think about any of my financial issues: my mounting credit-card debt, my student-loan debt, and my inability to make more money in journalism.

Still, the work itself was exciting. Every day was a new story. Every day meant going to a different location and talking to different people. But the job, distance from home, and cultural expectations to succeed exposed deep-seated insecurities and fears. I was living alone for the first time and all my friends and family were a ten-hour drive away. I shouldered the loneliness, insecurities, and my journalistic inadequacies by myself. Culture shock reared its head. At least in Seattle there was enough diversity where I didn't stick out. In Montana I felt like I was the only Asian guy in the entire state. The fear of racism, stereotypes, and teasing was paramount. Not only was I worrying about external perceptions of me, there were internal ones within my own culture I had to confront. My parents and relatives didn't want me in this profession. I felt a crushing sense of cultural responsibility to prove them wrong and uphold my family name as the oldest son and first family member in this country to receive a college degree. I wondered, What if I don't succeed in this career? Will my parents disown me? Will the wider Asian community back home reject me? I told myself that failure was not an option. The fear and potential shame of bringing dishonor to my Asian community, ancestors, and family weighed heavily on my conscience.

The anxiety that fueled these questions, doubts, and concerns swirled through my being. Even if I had wanted to talk about it, who could I turn to? This was before e-mail and cell phones. I had a landline, but I didn't have long-distance telephone service because I wanted to save money and chose isolation instead. The isolation sealed my distorted belief that I could not truly trust anyone in my deepest time of need. I would have to tackle these challenges alone.

Parents' traditional
Chinese Wedding
ceremony, Hong Kong

Sam as a toddler in Hong Kong

*Sam with childhood friend in Seattle*

*Sam celebrating 4th birthday in Hong Kong*

*Family at Snoqualmie Ski Summit outside Seattle.*
From left, *Sam;* middle, *Fred;* right, *Ken*

*Sam and his brothers with their mom in their Seattle home.*
From left, *Ken;* middle, *Sam;* right, *Fred*

Part II

# The American Addict

## Failure Is not an Option

My work in Montana as a beginning reporter was abysmal. My voice was high and my on-air presentation was amateurish at best. I was so nervous being on camera that I had the perpetual "deer caught in headlights" look. People would call the station after my live bloopers and say, "I love your newscast, but what happened to that Sam Louie?"

Additionally, I had limited knowledge of journalistic ethics. I would send an underage intern to buy alcohol at stores, thinking it would make a good story, only to end up in my boss's office, with him railing against the impropriety of doing so. Basically, if anything could go wrong in TV news, I did it.

My despair was so strong that I distinctly remember telling myself I'd be better off dead than returning home a failure. I vowed I could never face my family or community if I failed at this job. While the suicidal ideation was just a passing thought, there was a part of me that already had planned an exit strategy. I told myself I would relocate to San Francisco or another city with a large Asian population, so I could hide and avoid the familial and cultural shame of home if I quit my first job in journalism.

But the Chinese part of me was adamant that failure was not an option. The fear and potential shame of bringing dishonor to my family, grandparents, and deceased ancestors weighed too heavily on my conscience. I had to succeed. The anxiety that fueled these questions, doubts, and concerns swirled through my being. Being both a man and a person of Asian descent, talking about my concerns wasn't an option. This was never modeled to me and I thought real men just handled their issues on their own. I also internalized the American phrase "pull yourself up by the bootstraps." My emotional wall and internal isolation compounded my pre-existing, distorted beliefs that I was defective, inadequate, and bad, not just as a reporter but as a person. I now believe that my distorted views were the result of the strong Chinese values of obedience and honor. I was the disobedient son. I had defied my parents's wishes for me to become a teacher. I had done things without asking for permission, such as taking on my own paper route and skipping school. My sexual behaviors were disgraceful to my family name, even if they were unknown. The shame grew as the behaviors and associated feelings of fear, disappointment, and pain continued to swell.

## An Asian-American Journalist

Working in an industry in which I had no other Asian or ethnic journalists to connect with made it even more difficult. I hung out periodically with some of my coworkers, but my weekend schedule made it difficult. I remember the sports anchor and a few other staffers invited me to play a round of golf. As a poor Asian immigrant, I had not been exposed to the game, so even that invitation brought shame to me. It was one of the few opportunities to connect with some of my male colleagues, but it was something beyond what I could afford to learn or play. Why didn't they play a simple sport like basketball, where very little money was involved?

In my search for community, I learned of an organization known as the Asian-American Journalists Association (AAJA). This nonprofit, professional journalist association was founded in 1981 with the goal of supporting and encouraging more ethnic minorities, specifically Asians, to pursue a career in journalism.

That year, AAJA was holding its annual convention in Hawaii and I decided to plunge myself further in debt to attend. I had never been to a job-related convention nor set foot on an airplane, except when I first immigrated to the U.S. as a five-year-old. The anxiety of being on an airplane and the unknowns of attending a large convention among other peers for the first time were overwhelming. I went to the restroom at least a dozen times to urinate before we landed.

Despite those fears, I had signed up for the convention because the hope of meeting like-minded Asian-Americans offset my concerns. Maybe they could give me professional advice in this field and insight into how they navigated the internal pressures from their families, since journalism is not well-regarded in Asian households. It's not easy to go against your parents's wishes, so maybe I'd meet others who had done the same. During the next several days, I'd end up meeting a number of journalists who had similar cultural and professional struggles. It was so validating to hear stories from other Asian-American journalists who broke the mold. I had found a home where my ethnic and career aspirations intersected. Some of the peers I met through the organization more than two decades ago are still dear friends to this day.

While I was enjoying the emotional high of affirmation and support I got by attending the convention, when I returned to Montana the loneliness and fear set back in. I tried to distract myself from those negative feelings by playing as much pick-up basketball as I could during my off hours. But when I stopped playing, the ferocity of those fear-provoking feelings came forth. Never did I consider discussing them with my parents or friends, as that would signal weakness and shame on my part. I told myself, I am a man and I am not supposed to show vulnerability or feel fear. Yet the fear of failure gripped me. I struggled mightily to prevent those emotions from overwhelming and paralyzing me. I needed an outlet besides basketball. I needed a way out of this pain, something that would be dependable and pleasurable.

The answer was finding ways to get lost in sexual intrigue or fantasy. The isolation, fears, and loneliness proved to be a perfect storm for my eventual addiction to pornography.

## Hollywood Films to XXX Movies

In the beginning, I would rent traditional Hollywood movies at the local video store that had either intense kissing or brief nudity. Movies like *Basic Instinct* with Sharon Stone, *Wild Things* with Denise Richards, and *Indecent Proposal* with Demi Moore were enough to keep me satisfied. I would watch the movies from start to finish. My adrenaline would rise as the story arc culminated with sex or intense kissing. Oftentimes these scenes were too brief for me to pleasure myself, so I would replay them until I masturbated to orgasm. Afterwards, I would continue to watch until the end, rationalizing that because I watched the entire movie, I wasn't using it for sexual purposes.

But within a few months, I was getting sick and tired of replaying a minute or two of sexual material from these movies. So I gravitated to the B-movie section, where there were a plethora of films that combined sex with sinister plotlines of revenge, killings, and seductions. These movies had more nudity and longer scenes, but they also got annoying because they had plots that took time to reach the sexual content. It was also jarring because the sexuality was intertwined with guns and violence; one scene of sexuality could quickly splice with another of a man or woman getting killed. This did not provide the emotional safety I wanted for sexual fantasy and preoccupation. In other words, when I'm in a fantasy, the last thing I want is to see scenes of violence or death. But these movies were at least accessible and rentable through the local video store with limited shame. The thought of going to an adult video store with more explicit pornographic material both shamed and thrilled me. I was shamed because it seemed like such an admission of my weakness to cross this threshold of intent, yet it was also exciting to think of the possibilities.

Eventually I built up the courage to drive to the one adult video store in town. Along the way, I wondered what if someone recognized me. Would they call the station? Could I get fired for doing something like this on my days off? I didn't care anymore; the need for a sexual dopamine hit outweighed the risks.

When I went into the store, I was shocked that the clerk was female. This made me feel even more shame to have to interact with a woman. Wouldn't she think I was disgusting? I decided to make sure this was going to be a quick transaction. I averted her face and kept my eyes downward. Everything was a blur as I grabbed a few magazines within reach and paid for them. As the only Asian in town, I was worried either she or the customers in the store would recognize me. By the time I got in the car and drove away, I wondered why I was doing something I felt went against my values—such a contradiction and war between my mind and body. I didn't realize that pornography was becoming my emotional escape from the hardships of life. Instead, I rationalized that I was a guy with a high sex drive who needed it to quell his libido.

Once I had my stash of magazines, I looked at them nightly after work. Usually the ritual occurred after dinner and before bed as a way to wind down. I told myself that I needed to look at the images to help me get to sleep. I gravitated toward Caucasian women with brunette hair. This was what's known as my "arousal template," which is defined by author and doctor Patrick Carnes as "the total constellation of thoughts, images, behaviors, sounds, smells, sights, fantasies, and objects that arouse us sexually." I'm sure my arousal to white brunettes had a lot to do with my early attraction to the girls from middle school who treated me nicely and who I found attractive. White women were the standard of beauty, so part of me yearned for mainstream society's approval and acceptance, which I sought to project onto these women.

I wasn't the only one suffering sexually in my family. My mother called me out of the blue one day to ask for my help. She informed me that one of my younger brothers was straddled with more than $30,000 in credit-card debt from strip clubs and she wanted me to talk to him. I told my mom I would, since this was my duty as the oldest son. From as young as I can recall, my parents would remind me of the responsibility I had to be a good role model to my two younger brothers in this country. That talk with my brother never happened. There was no way I could entertain a conversation regarding strip clubs when I was suffering in a similar fashion. Oddly enough, when I heard about my brother's strip-club debt, I felt better about my own situation. He must be really out of control if he was paying for it and getting into serious debt. I saw my porn issue as small potatoes and manageable in comparison. At the time, it never occurred to me that our issues were interconnected, not due to randomness or chance. There was a reason we both had similar struggles. It just took therapy many years later for me to see it.

My brother's debt was never paid to the credit-card company. Shortly afterward, I learned he had decided to move to Japan ostensibly to teach English. It was a twofold decision: escape the creditors and be immersed in Asian culture. He told me he couldn't relate to white women here and felt being in Asia would give him a better chance of meeting women who might like him more. I thought it would be short-lived, but his move was permanent; he spent a number of years living in Japan, Hong Kong, and Singapore. He's never returned to the U.S. except for an occasional visit. And the credit-card companies never pursued him overseas.

## Breaking Up Is Easy to Do

During my time in Montana, I did have a brief, intense romance. A couple of my basketball buddies invited me out one night and we went to a few bars, where I met a woman who was a senior at the University of Montana. We clicked and soon became an item. She wanted to move in with me, but my friends warned against it. I had never met anyone who liked me this much and I confused intensity with intimacy. Two weeks after we met, she moved into my sparse apartment. It was an electric feeling having a girlfriend so interested in me. On weekdays she stayed at my apartment close to the university and on weekends we went to her parents's home. Her parents didn't blink when we slept in her bedroom. This made me nervous, but she tried to reassure me by saying, "My dad doesn't care what I do so long as he's aware of it." Despite her reassurances, I did my best to honor her parents by showing restraint when I was in their home.

When I was in this relationship, my porn use went down, so I never considered that I had an issue with it. But in hindsight, what I did was substitute porn with sex. I was using sex with her as a coping mechanism. The high of a sexual release drowned out any fears I had. I had no emotional intimacy. The only relationship I had was with the orgasm. Sex was compartmentalized and divorced from the relationship. I was so disconnected that when I got an offer to move to Ohio for my next position, I shed no tears in ending my relationship with her. I invited her out to dinner to celebrate my promotion and tell her we were done. I can still recall her crying when I shared the news. I was perplexed and dumbfounded and wondered why she was sad. I didn't share those same feelings. If anything, I thought to myself, nothing personal. It's just business.

Part of the disconnect was because of my own views of myself. I did not see myself as someone who could impact another person. I had spent my entire childhood trying to engage my parents in a real relationship, to no avail. As a result, I could not fathom my life actually meant something to anyone, let alone a woman I had known for only half a year. No one ever told me I was special and wanted. I saw myself as replaceable. Worse yet, that was how I also viewed her and other women in my life. I had no recognition of my own inherent worth. To believe I had value in her eyes would have challenged twenty-five years of my Asian upbringing. It was not something I could comprehend.

## Holy Toledo!

I flew from Missoula to Toledo to have a formal interview with the news director at the ABC station. When she told me my salary was going to be $22,000 the first year, I jumped for joy. I signed the contract and was eager for what awaited me, as I was now going to be a full-fledged reporter without having to lug around a heavy camera and tripod. I would be strictly reporting the news, no more videography or editing required. Ditching the need to be a "one-man-band" made me feel like a real reporter.

I left Montana and drove feverishly for the next twenty-seven hours, stopping only twice to sleep. The first night was in a cheap motel in South Dakota, where I could hear the banging of a headboard in the adjacent room, accompanied by moans and groans. The second night I intentionally stopped to sleep in South Bend, Indiana (two hours from Toledo), thinking I could give myself a rest from my breakneck pace and visit the University of Notre Dame. I had visions of leisurely soaking in the campus, taking pictures, and catching a glimpse of the iconic Golden Dome. When I woke up, though, my black-and-white thinking kicked in and I convinced myself that people wouldn't think I truly cared about my career if I deviated from going straight to Toledo. Thus I bypassed Notre Dame and when I arrived in Toledo I basked in pride for staying the course. I would later learn from my colleagues that the city was considered the armpit of Ohio and they found it amusing when they heard I was in such a rush to get there. Toledo was a gritty, industrial city with a history of manufacturing jobs. The crown jewel at the time was the Jeep factory, where the nation's Jeep Wranglers and Cherokees were made.

The economy and its blue-collar roots were often reflected in the stories we covered. I reported consistently on labor strikes, unions, and collective bargaining. Ethnically, there was a sizeable African-American community (27 percent), but the Asian population hovered at 1 percent. This did not instill confidence in helping me feel connected culturally. The racial anxiety only intensified during my first week at work when one of the anchors remarked, "Sam, do you know you're the first Asian person to walk through those doors?" Not only was I the first Asian to work at that station, I was the first Asian male to work in Toledo journalism (print, television, or radio). I was now trailblazing not just for me and my family legacy, but also shouldering the weight of other Asian-American journalists. I felt an extra burden to do well so I wouldn't tarnish or negatively impact the opportunities of aspiring Asian-American journalists.

Living more than 2,000 miles away from Seattle, in a city bereft of any friends, family, or cultural connection, was terrifying. After making some friends in Montana, I had to start the process all over in Toledo: find an apartment, meet new coworkers, learn new skills in journalism, and try to build community. Anxiety and insecurity quickly set in. The responsibilities increased while grace for on-air gaffes decreased. When working in much smaller cities, there's an understanding that on-air reporters and anchors are just starting off and are given significant leeway in their on-air presentation. In Montana I went on live TV only a couple of times. Once was a feature story for the summer carnival and the other was a hostage standoff where the suspect killed himself rather than surrender to police. Regardless of whether it was a fun or serious story, I nearly peed my pants on both occasions.

In a bigger city like Toledo, the expectation was daily live news reporting, multiple times a day. Instead of seeing it as an opportunity to grow and learn, my shame spiraled every time I made a pronunciation error, forgot my lines, or had to ad-lib, which was my worst skill set. I would overhear my cohorts snicker when a fellow reporter or anchor made mistakes. Beyond my own shame, there were coworkers I had to be wary of, as they could also target me for my on-air inadequacies. On a racial note, it seemed a few of my white colleagues would delight even more when the mistakes were made by our Black coworkers. I heard murmurs and snide remarks that these staff members were hired because of their race. If race wasn't made explicit before, it was now rearing its ugly head, front and center.

The scorn was due to what I believe is the unfortunate fact that minorities are often judged differently in the workplace. If you're white and do a poor job at work, your performance is the only aspect that's criticized or considered. Race is never factored in for a white person's poor work ethic, integrity, or performance. How often do you hear, "John's a horrible and lazy employee. Why did we hire him? Was it because he's white?" But as an ethnic minority, it's open season to have people question whether you were a "token" hire to meet some ethnic quota.

For myself, with so much at stake in proving my worth to all parties involved, I needed something to take away the edge. During my time in Toledo, the internet was in its nascent, dial-up phase. That ubiquitous trilling sound of the modem connecting to the internet made my pulse quicken and my heart beat faster, knowing that pornography was now just a few keystrokes and mouse clicks away. Despite the long download times and pixelated imagery, it was a means to easily obtain an unlimited supply of free pornography without the fear of public exposure. I was hooked on porn like a crack addict. I couldn't wait to get home from work and get into fantasy. The thrill was spending the time searching for the perfect image. It had to be just right before I felt I could masturbate. The way the woman looked in the camera, the way I imagined she felt for me—all had to be the way I wanted it to be before I felt I could finish the job. Even if I found the right image early on, I would search for at least an hour or two to ensure she was the correct one. I couldn't just masturbate to any nude image. The brunette's hair length, stature, pose, and breast size (not too small, not too large) all had to be the way I envisioned it, before I felt it was acceptable to end the search and move on to the final phase of completion. After orgasm, I felt such a wave of relief and surrender. It was a physical and mental bliss that allowed me to function through the dreariness of life.

It was my one ray of sunshine in those dark moments of anxiety and discouragement.

But as exhilarating and euphoric as this was for me, it also brought waves of depression and shame. I hated myself, and my dependency on it was a self-fulfilling prophecy that I was a despicable and worthless person.

I was so alone in Toledo, a city that was very Black and white in its demographics. Once again, where were the Asians? I played basketball five days a week after work, as I considered the court my safe place. Outside of basketball, the computer became my safe place. Whenever I felt even a twinge of insecurity or homesickness, I found porn could take it all away, even if it was temporary.

When I wasn't looking at online pornography, I'd troll the bars and dance clubs looking for real women. It really didn't matter who she was or whether we had any shared interests so long as she wanted to hook up. I dated a white nurse for a couple of months. Ironically, she was a smoker. I hated the smell of smoke, but I felt it was better to be with anyone than alone. My bar for relationships was low; if you wanted to be with me that's all that mattered. The relationship with the nurse didn't last long, as I think we both realized we didn't care for anything but hooking up. When she broke up with me, I was upset. I was the one to break up with women in the past and this change in the pattern made me question my Asian masculinity even more. I took it personally that white women didn't like Asian guys, and I reverted back to internet porn.

I also had access to a large stash of *Playboy* magazines at another job I worked to make ends meet. Since I was the morning reporter, my shift ended around one p.m. and I worked as a caregiver at a group home with three men with mental and developmental disabilities. I helped them cook meals, ensured that they took their medications, and took them on outings occasionally.

One of them had schizophrenia and would get angry and hostile, yelling and lashing out at whoever was around him. This terrified me and I tried to avoid him as much as possible. Another was bound to a wheelchair and had extremely dry skin and I had to rub lotion on his feet. The third was developmentally delayed and needed my help accessing art supplies, as he drew nude pictures of women. When I asked where the inspiration came from, he showed me the private collection of *Playboy* magazines he kept in one of his drawers. I thought I hit pay dirt when he showed it to me. When it was dinnertime, I put on their favorite show and knew I'd have thirty minutes to myself. I'd sneak into his dresser and grab a magazine or two and masturbate in the bathroom. It was the perfect scenario. I was able to access the magazines undetected and I was getting paid to do so! After that discovery, I couldn't wait to go to their home. I was a caretaker for those three men and was taking care of myself at the same time.

## 'Hi, I Work for ABC News!'

Despite working in a city with no longtime friends or family close by, the television news industry provided some camaraderie and community. Some of us single coworkers would band together and go out to explore the city. One night we went to an upscale jazz club, where I saw a young Asian couple. They were the first Asians I had come across in nearly two years and my desire for a connection was too strong to hold back. Without hesitation, I bolted from our table and made a beeline to them. I never considered this act could be viewed as intrusive or threatening to the Asian guy (i.e. trying to hit on his girlfriend). In my mind, I needed to bond with other Asians, even if it may come across as a bit bold.

After some chitchat, I learned both of them grew up in Toledo and were Korean-American. They weren't dating, but had simply gone to a wedding together since they were both single. I told them I was somewhat new to the city and gestured to the ABC News lapel on my blazer hoping they'd be impressed. I fudged the facts a bit and told them I was an on-air reporter with ABC when technically I was a reporter for the local ABC affiliate. Neither watched TV news so the ruse didn't matter.

By the time my friends were ready to leave, I wanted to ensure that I didn't lose my one Asian connection. I asked for both of their numbers and later that week I called "Sara" and asked her out on a date for the upcoming weekend. I was smitten with her and, instead of a typical date of going out, I wanted to do something special for her. I didn't typically cook much back then, but thought she'd be worth the effort. I even called my parents to ask for a Chinese chicken recipe (chicken with black-bean sauce). I scribbled down the recipe and tested it out that week and invited a coworker over to see if it would pass the muster. He liked it, but suggested I also include a salad and dessert, since he noticed I hadn't even considered anything but the main course.

When the time came for the date, I was abuzz with nervous energy. This was my one shot to impress an Asian woman. I had never even considered dating an Asian during my journalism journey, but maybe the yearning for similarity took hold. I also was "once bitten, twice shy" after my most recent break-up with my white girlfriend and was apprehensive of dating a white woman again.

Apparently, I couldn't get over this rejection. During dinner, I couldn't stop blathering about my bitterness toward and rejection by white women. Sara didn't think it was a good idea to continue with a second date; she didn't feel I was emotionally ready. I pleaded with her to give me another chance and swore to no longer talk about my past relationships, but instead focus on us, to which she agreed.

Sara and I were sexual from the start. It didn't take long before we were having sex every time we saw each other. I viewed this as a good thing, since I could tell myself I didn't need porn and it was just a passing fad while I was waiting for the real thing.

The first couple of months felt like bliss. I was ecstatic I wasn't alone anymore and it felt great that I wasn't using porn. Not only that, she and I had our shared Asian background. Yet I soon discovered that commonality wasn't good enough for her parents. She did not tell her parents she was dating me, primarily because I was not Korean. I was naïve and didn't think Asians could have an issue dating each other, since all the various Asians I grew up with in Seattle got along. But I soon learned getting along as friends or classmates is one thing; dating someone outside your ethnicity is another. When she did share my background with her parents, they told her she would have to end the relationship.

I was crestfallen—first rejection by white women, now rejection from someone I thought was my own kind. I felt intense shame for being Chinese. In a last-gasp attempt to keep it from ending, I proposed meeting her parents face-to-face and if they still found me wanting I'd be willing to walk away from the relationship. This was quite a bold move on my part, because beyond the cultural difference there was also a socioeconomic and educational gulf between our families. My parents were restaurant workers with a limited education that ended as early as middle school. Sara's parents were affluent and educated in the United States. Her father had a PhD in engineering and her mother a master's degree in education. Her older sister was a pediatrician in Chicago and Sara had graduated from Northwestern and was a successful commercial realtor. Her family lived in the most exclusive area in Toledo and owned a few apartment complexes and amassed a large amount of wealth through passive income. It looked like their family took to heart the message of the book *Rich Dad Poor Dad* by Robert Kiyosaki, where true wealth is accrued not by a job but through business ownership.

## Guess Who's Coming to Dinner?

When I met Sara's parents it was intimidating, as I had never been to an affluent neighborhood before, let alone a home within one. The neighborhood of Ottawa Hills, where they lived, boasts multimillion-dollar homes, with the majority of them having more than eight rooms. Theirs was no different. If anything, it was even more impressive, as they had a full-sized tennis court in the backyard. I thought the only thing missing was the white-picket fence.

Once inside, they greeted me warmly and ushered me to a seat in their dining room. We started with Korean appetizers and, during the course of the next two hours, they asked numerous questions regarding my background to see if I met their standards to date their daughter. I winced when they asked about my parents's jobs, but I had been coached by Sara to accentuate their professions. My dad magically went from a cook at a mediocre Chinese restaurant to a chef at a popular, high-end Asian-fusion eatery. As for my mother, I told them she worked in the "medical field" and said, due to my lack of ability to speak Chinese, I didn't really understand the nature of her work. In reality, she was part of the immigrant labor force that cleaned the medical supplies at a hospital. But Sara's marching orders were to keep my mom's job description vague, as her parents would be aghast if they knew the truth. I could feel the essence of my identity slowly seeping out of me with every lie I told. There was already plenty of shame in me prior to this, but it felt like it went even deeper. The core of my being was woefully inadequate. The inadequacy was not limited just to me, but included my parents and, by extension, my Chinese heritage. Everything I was I interpreted as not being good enough.

But I did what I thought I had to do knowing they were vetting me, and my relationship with Sara hung in the balance. They clung to their ethnic dream that their daughter would be courted by a Korean and, in the midst of the dinner, I got the sense I didn't have much to offer their daughter. I quickly pivoted and decided to lean heavily on what I did have at the time: my perceived celebrity status as a television news reporter.

I was going to swap out their ethnic dream of having their daughter marry a Korean with the dream that their daughter could be with an on-air personality. Once the discussion focused on my job and my potential, it felt like the momentum shifted to

Team Louie. Her parents were fastidious when it came to current events. They hadn't seen me on local news, as they preferred watching national network news programs. One show they were acutely aware of and mentioned since I worked at the ABC affiliate was *Nightline* (ABC's in-depth, late-night news show hosted then by Ted Koppel). They asked if that was a possible destination for me. I nodded in affirmation and told them with hard work and persistence anything was possible: *Nightline, Dateline, 20/20, The Today Show*. With this prospect of my potential to be a household name, Dr. and Mrs. "Kim" began to take a keen interest in me. If anything, they began effusively encouraging their daughter to date me.

But these professional aspirations weren't my true desires, so it felt like the vise was closing quickly on how honest I could be with them and those around me. My reality was always to work on a more feature-related show like *Entertainment Tonight* or *Access Hollywood*. But I knew what they liked and didn't want to rock the proverbial boat, so I just felt it was best to keep stoking this fantasy of being a "serious news reporter," lest I jeopardize my blossoming relationship with Sara.

It didn't take long for them to welcome me with open arms. In return, I was just as excited to play my part to join an affluent Korean family. I felt I was living an Asian version of the TV show *Lifestyles of the Rich and Famous*, with the country-club memberships, lavish dinners, and vacations to Florida and Mexico. I promised to learn the Korean language and practiced it at every opportunity, even between live reports. I also took golf lessons for the first time and at one point diligently practiced up to three hours a day so I could be seen as proficient. If only my Montana coworkers could see me now. Who knew I'd be playing golf at two country clubs? I saw the allure of golf beyond the game. It's a genteel sport where success, privilege, and leisure intersect. It was odd, as the staff of the clubs knew all the members's names and waited on us hand and foot. We would eat nice meals and I was filled with polarizing feelings—a twinge of guilt coupled with a sense of entitlement. I felt entitled to be treated with respect, due to being an affiliate member of the country club, yet there was guilt, as I felt I was abandoning my blue-collar roots by seeing the staff at these places as nonentities, merely servants at our disposal.

Sara's family was everything my family was not: wealthy, educated, relational, and religious. While Dr. and Mrs. Kim were immigrants from South Korea, they were highly educated and spoke English well. In this sense, it was like being in a family I had always envisioned. Talking to parents in a language we could both understand without anything getting lost in translation was quite different from what I was used to growing up. They also understood my career journey (i.e. having to move to find work), whereas my parents didn't understand how to navigate corporate America. If anything, they thought it was stupid for me to move, asking quizzically, "Why aren't you working here, since there are four TV stations in Seattle?"

Sara's family was also very tight-knit. Mrs. Kim was especially nurturing. She would joke with me in a loving way and treated me like the son they never had. Sara's older sister, Jenny, was very empathetic. She was a pediatrician in Chicago and married to Joe, a Korean-American who worked as a money manager for a financial-brokerage firm. Sara would periodically tell me she always thought her sister could have done better. I was confused because I had thought being Korean was good enough, but quickly learned that your profession defines you as much as your ethnic background. This spiked my anxiety because Joe looked like the poster child for Korean masculinity and attractiveness: a good job, a business degree from a prestigious university, fluent in Korean. All I had compared to him was a job in television news. Didn't that pale in comparison?

But my job title was my calling card to acceptance. Everywhere we went they gushed and introduced me to their friends: "Please meet our daughter's boyfriend. He's a TV news reporter!" Their association with me gave them an extra sense of prestige they used to differentiate themselves from other successful Koreans.

The luster of my job title was intoxicating to them and to me. I drank it in as often as I could, knowing I could do no wrong with this identity as my badge of honor and shield against criticism.

After two years of dating Sara, I wasn't sure what to do. I had mixed feelings. I received an offer to work at the ABC station in Cincinnati, which was a three-hour drive away. My pattern of breaking up and moving on tugged at me. Yet the fear of loneliness and the cultural and familial connection I made with Sara and her family made me think twice. I went against my instincts and decided I would propose to her without informing my parents. Sara made sure I went through the proper steps with her family, though, and had gotten her parents's blessing to do so.

As I continued to project myself to them as a perfect, future son-in-law, the reality was starting to close in on me and I wasn't sure what to do. No one knew I was viewing porn via magazines, DVDs, and the internet. If anything, the professional expectations to make it to the network and fit into the Korean mold increased my porn usage to multiple times a day, lasting a couple of hours each time. I dared not utter a word about this, even to my fiancée.

## Premarital Counseling: Watch More Porn?

Premarital counseling was suggested to start our marriage on the right track. Since Sara and I belonged to a church, we knew a retired psychologist who was willing to do the counseling as a free service to the community. The counseling took place in one of the church offices. The psychologist asked me and Sara about our family backgrounds and individual and shared values to see if there were any areas of conflict. We talked about our socioeconomic, educational, and ethnic differences, but told him we had sorted it all out.

Midway through the session, he asked us if there was anything else that he should know that might be helpful in his work with us. At this prompting, I took a deep breath, exhaled, and muttered something to the effect of, "I look at stuff." Upon further probing from the psychologist, I nonchalantly said, "I sometimes look at pictures and videos of naked women." Sara looked shell-shocked. My image as a clean-cut, nice, Christian man was quickly being torn down. She glanced at the psychologist for guidance. To our surprise, he didn't think there was much of a problem. In fact, he suggested I "do more porn" as a means to flood my system and rid my interest in it once and for all before getting married. I heeded his "prescription" and Sara thought I was cured. Meanwhile, my behavior continued unabated.

## Another Name Change

Before our marriage, Sara insisted that I would have to replace my Chinese last name with her Korean one. We reached a compromise of sorts, where I agreed to drop my middle name in exchange for her family's Korean name. Sam Fu Yuen Louie would no longer exist. The new version was Sam Kim Louie. Furthermore, she requested that if we had children, the boys could carry her family name (Kim) and the girls could reflect my Chinese name (Louie). Sara wanted to ensure her family name was honored. I believe this had a lot to do with her own feelings of inadequacy. She confided to me that her parents were disappointed she wasn't born a boy to pass down the family name and now here was her opportunity to ensure the legacy would continue in the next generation. I was torn. I could tell my parents and close friends were incredulous. But I reluctantly agreed, as I sensed this was non-negotiable for her. In retrospect, this agreement was born of codependency and fear. I was fearful she'd leave me if I disagreed, so I told myself marriage was about sacrifice and this was one of those sacrifices I'd have to make to please my wife.

## WKRP in Cincinnati

Another sacrifice I made was moving to Cincinnati alone while Sara and I were engaged. I got a better-paying job in a larger television market and we both understood work took priority.

We agreed I would live there alone for the first six months until we got married and she had time to phase out of her job as a commercial real estate agent. On the weekends, I would make the three-hour drive back to Toledo as often as possible to be with her and my soon-to-be in-laws. In the meantime, I had to figure out Cincinnati on my own.

Being a reporter in Cincinnati felt surreal. As a child, I watched the television sitcom *WKRP in Cincinnati*. Now it felt like life was imitating art. I could never have imagined that someone from my immigrant background would end up in this city working on the air. I had made it! I was working in a legitimate big city with a MLB and NFL team. It was also home to Procter and Gamble and a few other Fortune 500 companies.

I worked for WCPO-TV and we had all the tools needed for the trade: numerous trucks that allowed us to broadcast live, a satellite truck in case we needed to transmit beyond the city, and even our own news helicopter. My colleagues were impressive. Many had garnered journalism's top recognition, the Edward R. Murrow Awards, and regional Emmy Awards. They were known commodities in the community, as some had worked at the station for more than twenty years. This was not Missoula or Toledo, where you honed your craft and then moved to a larger city. Cincinnati was a destination where coworkers relished their jobs and understood the nature of their work. The main anchor at the time was a well-respected African-American man who oozed charm, professionalism, and humor. The white colleagues never said anything negative about him. If anything, his command of the anchor desk and knowledge of local and international politics made others genuinely accept that he had earned his position as the highest paid employee at the station. This wasn't what I was used to coming from all the white jealousy and animosity in Toledo. As for their treatment of me, everyone was very welcoming.

But no matter how welcoming they were, it still couldn't change that I was once again the lone Asian reporter in the entire

Cincinnati media market. The pressure to do well for myself and my family continued unabated.

But I was doing all right, all things considered. My skills on-air were passable, except for a handful of times. Once I went to do a live report in our station's helicopter and my voice trembled and I couldn't concentrate. I was not only motion-sick but stumbling on my words, as my earpiece was echoing whatever I said. My boss was not pleased and asked to speak to me in his office afterwards. I was worried what this conversation meant. Was my job in jeopardy if I screwed up again on-air? Another time I was covering a court-related story and was to go live at noon with an update. I didn't understand at the time what was happening in the courtroom and yet I had to give a short and succinct report. I made up something on the spot and just spat it out when the anchor called my name on the air. It felt terrible to have no understanding of the story but to explain it confidently like I was well-versed in it. Talk about presenting a public image that's much different from my internal experience.

These work conflicts were related to my own personal ones, as I was using porn all the time to deal with the fear of getting fired.

Performance anxiety is real. One evening during a major news story, my mind simply went blank when I was on the air. I couldn't recall what I was supposed to say, and the anchor came to the rescue and summarized my report for the audience. I went home and crumpled into a fetal position and wanted to stay there forever. I did not want to face the scrutiny of my boss or my colleagues. Obviously, my boss was unhappy and my colleagues also reinforced that I had to do better, as there was no room for those types of egregious mistakes, especially since we were the top-rated station in the city.

## The Big Apple and the City of Angels

As soon as Sara joined me in Cincinnati, she was ready to leave. It had nothing to do with me and everything to do with her. With no desire to start over as a realtor knowing we could move again for my career, she decided she wanted to pursue a career in acting. As a codependent, new husband who was I to object? Shouldn't I be supportive of her interests? Since Cincinnati wasn't a hotbed for actors, she was determined to go to New York City. I reluctantly agreed to a long-distance relationship so she could move to New York to follow her passion. I told myself marriage was about sacrifice, already having given up my Chinese middle name. How much more difficult would it be to sacrifice the normalcy of having your spouse living with you?

My salary was close to $40,000, but most of it went to pay for our rent and living expenses in two different cities. A long-distance marriage is hard enough, let alone trying to do it as newlyweds. But that was my lot in life and I knew how to cope with it. I found solace by playing pick-up basketball at the local YMCA and, of course, in internet pornography. I was numb to whatever criticism came my way at work or in my marriage. The isolation and loneliness was punctured by the occasional weekend when I drove to Toledo to visit my in-laws or when Sara flew to Cincinnati.

After nearly two years of working in Cincinnati, I got a call from a news director in Los Angeles to come work for his station. The news director had been a mentor of sorts and was delighted to see my newsreel among the hundreds vying for the coveted position. It was a dream come true. My wife and I could finally be reunited, Sara could continue to act, and I could work in one of the biggest media markets in the U.S. with the support of a boss who I had looked up to for a number of years.

## Indecent Proposal

When I attended my first journalism convention in Hawaii, I met a news director from Los Angeles who I connected with. "Terry" was someone I looked up to professionally and personally. He was tall, well-dressed, respected, and handsome. I thought he was the epitome of a lady's man. I couldn't believe someone in his position would be interested in my small-town work, but he gave me advice, encouragement, and support that I desperately needed.

I distinctly remember a time at a silent auction at the convention when Terry saw a book I was interested in and decided to outbid everyone for it. A woman who also wanted the book wondered who would place a $100 bid on a book worth twenty dollars, and Terry said, "I did it because it's for Sam!" That moment made me feel cherished. It touched a very deep part of me that felt wanted.

Terry would occasionally call me to see how I was doing and he was the one person I was honest with regarding my pessimism about my talent. He allayed my concerns by saying everyone goes through these moments of self-doubt and that I would get better with time. When I moved to Toledo and met Sara, I lost touch with him, until I applied for the reporter position in Los Angeles. I had no idea it was the same station where he was in charge. After receiving my résumé reel, he flew me out to Los Angeles for an interview. I was nervous, as it brought up similar feelings to my interview at McDonald's when I was a teenager. What would he ask me? How do I prepare for this interview? Would he ask me a number of trivia questions about L.A. that I would need to know?

I arrived in time for the morning newsroom meeting, where the producers and managers discussed which news stories they wanted covered that day and which reporters would be the best fit for each story. After the meeting, I spent time with some of the management and they shared their roles and responsibilities with me and also what they loved about living and working in Los Angeles.

The first night I went to dinner with one of the managers and was still waiting for someone to conduct a formal interview with me. Maybe this manager would do it over the appetizers, I thought, but it never happened. The few questions I do recall him asking were related to cars and women. "What do you like to drive?" "What type of women do you like?" He shared that he loved Los Angeles since there were so many "leggy" women in the city. I told him I drove a Honda Accord and he replied, "Hondas are good cars!" I told him I was married and only had eyes for my wife, and he said, "Good for you, man."

The next day I spent with Terry in his office, where he talked more about the benefits of working in L.A. I was bracing for him to steer the conversation into an interview and ask me questions like why I thought I deserved this job over others or something like that. But when it never happened, I began feeling guilty. Why didn't I have to go through an interview? I knew Terry, but that shouldn't have given me an advantage over other hardworking reporters who also wanted this job. I was naïve and it took a few more hours before it dawned on me that this was a done deal since Terry knew me, liked me, and wanted me there. The adage of "it's not what you know, but who you know" was becoming a personal truth for me.

On my last night in L.A., Terry, my long-time mentor and future boss asked if I'd like to eat at Morton's Steakhouse in Beverly Hills. I was giddy because Beverly Hills felt like a fantasy world I had seen only on TV. Terry told me to meet him at his place beforehand, as he would be driving us to the restaurant. When I arrived, he was already busy making apple martinis to start off the night. After the first one, he encouraged me to drink another, but I told him I don't drink much due to what's colloquially known as the "Asian flu." (Many Asians lack the enzyme to digest alcohol and get an allergic reaction when they drink.)

In Morton's, I was impressed by the professionalism of the staff and their treatment of my mentor. They knew him by name. During our dinner, he ordered a bottle of wine to complement the meal and insisted I drink with him. After the entrée, he ordered dessert wine. I didn't want to disappoint him, so I continued drinking, even though I was starting to feel sick. On the ride back to his condo, he asked if I wanted to see what nightlife looked like in Los Angeles. He asked if I had any objections to going to a gay club and I said no, not understanding the implications of my decisions.

He held my hand as we walked into the club. I was perplexed. Do I allow this to continue or do I tell him I am uncomfortable? Due to the fear of reprisal, I let him hold my hand as he guided me upstairs to a more private section, where we sat on a sofa. He then began kissing my neck, and my whole body stiffened, unsure of what to do. This continued for a few more minutes and then I asked if I could go back to my hotel, as I had to catch an early flight to Ohio the next morning.

While driving me to my hotel, Terry urged me to return to his condo for more drinks. I told him I could not drink any more. He looked at me with severe disapproval and disappointment. I didn't know what to do. If I left immediately, would my job prospect at his station disappear? If I agreed, would he think I was acquiescing to him sexually? It felt like a scene from the movie *Indecent Proposal*. But instead of trading sex for money, sex with my mentor meant solidifying a job as a news reporter in one of the media capitals of the world. I couldn't jeopardize losing such an amazing career opportunity, so I agreed to enter his condo. I told him I would not be drinking and steeled myself mentally, in case he tried to force himself on me. I told myself, If he tries to force himself on you, you need to fight back!

We sat on his couch and he began kissing my neck again and rubbing my chest. He kept telling me he "loved me" and requested that I take off my pants, at which point I recoiled and left his condo, thinking my opportunity to work in L.A. was over.

I slept three hours at the hotel, before it was time to catch a taxi to the airport. My head was throbbing from the alcohol and, as the taxi driver drove me to LAX, he stopped a few times so I could vomit. I was stuck in the bathroom for most of the flight, trying to vomit out the alcohol, but nothing would come out because I was dehydrated. Arriving in Ohio, I was taken to the emergency room, where I spent the next twenty-four hours on Christmas Eve hooked up to an IV, recovering from alcohol poisoning.

Afterward, I thought over the events in anguish. Had Terry been grooming me all these years? Was his desire to hire me just a ploy to get into my pants? I was horrified, embarrassed, and unable to answer the questions from Sara and her side of the family. Why hadn't I just said no to drinking? Why had I gone along with his advances? They wondered if I was a gay man living a secret life. There was no understanding that my problem was I was codependent and didn't know how to say no.

I later learned in therapy that I had never felt I had the right to say no. I was culturally taught to "listen and obey." I was not allowed to speak back nor did I see myself as someone who had a voice that mattered in this world.

## The Phone Conversation

A few days after I returned to Ohio, Terry and I spoke on the phone.

"Sam!" he said. "You got back OK?"

"Um," I uttered. "Not really. I had to be hospitalized because of alcohol poisoning."

"You're kidding? Why didn't you stop drinking?"

"I tried! I kept telling you I couldn't drink anymore, remember? I had to be hospitalized because I couldn't retain any liquids. They put an IV in me so my fluids could come back to normal."

"Oh God, Sam. That's horrible. We obviously had too much."

"All these years we built up trust and I just don't know if I am being hired on merit or if there are any other intentions. I tried to tell you it was uncomfortable and awkward, and I allowed some things to happen probably because you're. ... I would not have allowed any of that to happen with anybody else."

Terry was adamant that he wasn't trying to take advantage of me. "No way! No way were there other intentions. Absolutely not! I think it was Mr. Alcohol speaking and I'm very sorry about that. I thought, Here we are. It's an adventure and you seemed to be okay with it. You know what. I'd like to put this behind us, if we can?"

I shrugged my shoulders and eked out "okay" in resignation.

I can now see how Terry reframed the narrative as one where "we" drank too much and "we" did things that were regrettable.

Never did he take personal accountability or responsibility for taking advantage of me. But then again, why would he? He knew he was in the wrong, but he also knew he had a naïve and vulnerable person who he could manipulate.

Like many sexual-assault victims, I downplayed his actions and rationalized that because I wasn't raped nothing serious had occurred. But it's clear this was someone taking advantage of the power differential between us.

## 'I Didn't Think I Could Say No'

Once out of the hospital, I had a powwow with Sara's family to discuss my options. Sara, her parents, sister, and brother-in-law were all gathered in the living room and asked me a number of pointed questions. They all seemed perplexed by my general response—"I didn't think I could say no"—but agreed it was no use looking backwards and to focus on the future.

I quickly forgave Terry. My dream of working in the Los Angeles media market along with Sara's dream of being an actor was too enticing to forgo. The only change to the plan was asking Terry to reduce my contract from three years to two. Sara and I thought this would give us flexibility if we decided my work environment was intolerable.

Sara was excited to move to Los Angeles, as she had never lived on or even visited the West Coast. Our marriage seemed to stabilize, and I played the role of successful TV reporter for her and her family. My porn habit was never discussed. After the premarital counseling, she never asked how I was doing in that department and I didn't bring up my struggles. It was an area of my life waiting to be exposed.

## 'Sam, You Suck!'

The physical touching by Terry stopped, but the emotional and psychological abuse was just beginning. During my tenure under his supervision, he would consistently call me into his office and tell me I would never measure up to the other reporters. Everything from my voice to my looks to my writing was unsatisfactory in his eyes. One time he played a recent news report of mine and after about twenty seconds he paused the video and said, "Sam, you suck!" I had endured a number of these meetings before without an emotional dent, but this time I started crying in his office. When I cracked, I think he believed he could manipulate me any way he wanted. For starters, he made me take weekly voice lessons. The voice coach he recommended charged $200 an hour. His advice to improve my vocal quality included pulling on my tongue as a warm-up and taking off my pants prior to recording any of my story narrations as a way to "free" me from restrictions. The photographers who witnessed this thought it was ludicrous, but, once again, it really had nothing to do with my voice and everything to do with power and control. The psychological abuse of making me feel small and unworthy kept Terry in control.

All of this impacted me deeply. I struggled with self-esteem. Terry's insults and manipulation left me in a fragile emotional state. I believed I wasn't good enough for the L.A. market and was only hired for his sexual gratification. I was haunted by what he thought of me. I yearned for his praise, but got only scorn and criticism. I felt helpless at work, but didn't dare confide in my coworkers.

I also felt like I had no control at home. Even though I was making six figures and working in Los Angeles, I still felt inadequate. Sara took care of all the finances and would explain to me we were losing money every month. How could I be making the most money of my career and still come up short? She said that her acting classes, beauty products, and other acting-related services were costing a lot of money, but I just internalized it as being not good enough for her. I wondered if I would ever be good enough in her eyes.

Sara and I were like ships passing in the night. I worked a swing shift and she was usually asleep when I returned home. The fear of being viewed as weak, insecure, or inadequate made it difficult to share with her any fears or concerns I had with my colleagues, boss, or on-air performance. Once again I reverted to playing pick-up basketball and to daily masturbation to online pornography. But it wasn't just relegated to my home computer. At work I had a private office and I accessed porn after my shift.

## The Playboy Reporter

Sara often watched the nightly newscast and gave constructive feedback on my stories. Beyond my performance, she verbalized being uncomfortable with my assignments, as I was often sent to cover stories at the Playboy Mansion, the lingerie store Frederick's of Hollywood, and other sexually themed locations. Ironically, Terry thought it was funny when I would try to get out of assignments that I felt were too sexually alluring. The UPN station I worked for considered "Playmate of the Year" or "Lingerie Model of the Month" newsworthy, as the station was geared toward a young, male audience since WWE Wrestling preceded some of our newscasts.

I told Terry about my wife's concerns and he laughed. Instead of helping me on the home front, he seemed to relish having the news producers assign even more provocative stories to me. Not only did this infuriate Sara further, it got the other male reporters upset at me. The photographers would confide to me that a number of the reporters thought I was getting preferential treatment. I was assigned to cover anything that occurred at the Playboy Mansion so frequently that it became comical. Young men would randomly come up to me at Rite-Aid or the local grocery store and quip, "Hey, man. Aren't you the Playboy reporter?"

The photographers enjoyed covering these stories and would often ask to be assigned to me. When we did end up at the Playboy Mansion, I'd avert my eyes if I saw nudity. When they asked me what was wrong, I replied I was a married man trying to uphold my vows. Some laughed and thought I was a eunuch, while others tried to persuade me nothing was wrong with sneaking a peek. "You can look at the menu, but you just can't order" was a common refrain. Little did they know I had been hooked on all things sensual for more than twenty years dating back to my childhood and was trying to not make things worse. But things were getting worse on the home front, as I stopped initiating sex with Sara because she would often reject my advances. It was unclear at the time, but many times when I tried to touch her, she would feel uncomfortable or agitated. Little did either of us know this had to do with her past sexual trauma, which she would learn later in therapy. In my head, I decided if I viewed porn I wouldn't have to bother her with my pesky sexual requests.

My ritual started when I got off work. Since I worked the late-night newscast, I would return from the field to the station around 11 p.m. and write a follow-up story on my work computer. Since I had my own private office on the second floor, I sometimes used the computer to look at porn, but usually I would go home and do so. Whether it was at work or home, I told myself I deserved a reward for a hard day's work. The stress of live TV news, my boss, and my wife's lack of sexual desire all fed into my justifications.

Home was the safest outlet, as Sara would be asleep by the time I got back to our Hollywood apartment. I would scroll through free porn sites, scouring for what I considered the "perfect image." Since my arousal fantasy centered on brunettes, every night presented another opportunity to hunt for new pornographic prey. Being in Los Angeles also exposed me to celebrities, and looking for nude pictures of actresses I had interviewed or seen in movies added to the excitement. From start to finish, the ritual usually lasted two hours. I had a cleansing ritual as well. I would take a small washcloth and use it to clean my body. It also acted as a psychological purge—I mentally cleansed myself of the shame.

## 'Thank God, I'm Caught!'

One late night while I was in my ritualistic trance of looking at online pornography, Sara woke up to use the restroom. She peered into the living room and saw what I was doing. A shriek of disgust pierced the air. I felt my heart drop into the pit of my stomach. She immediately demanded answers. How long have you been doing this? Are you seeing anyone else? Am I not good enough for you? I tried to reassure her that it had nothing to do with her and everything to do with me, but she viewed my behavior as a betrayal and told me so.

I felt exposed, helpless, alone, and afraid. At the same time there was strangely also relief. Thank God! I thought. I can stop living a double life. Finally, someone knew my secret. It had been exposed during pre-marital counseling, but I continued going back to porn without anyone else knowing. The secrecy was burdensome, and it had finally come to an end. I could not hide behind denials or rationalizations. I had to acknowledge to my wife and myself that the tentacles of pornography and sexual objectification of women had strangled the intimacy of our marriage. I could also finally acknowledge I was a porn and sex addict, which I wasn't able to do when we had gotten engaged just a couple of years earlier.

Sara and I immediately separated, since she wanted time to think. We saw a marriage therapist for a handful of sessions before Sara decided to discontinue the sessions. She explained that she now realized she had a lot of past sexual trauma to work through and didn't have the bandwidth to deal with more of it from our marriage. She shared how she was sexually molested repeatedly by an uncle when she was around ten years old. Additionally she was date-raped in college. I knew none of this during our relationship, but it now made sense why there was such sexual aversion. My sexual betrayal was the final straw. In the ensuing months, we were officially divorced.

The feelings of loss, abandonment, and shame associated with my divorce under these circumstances were excruciating. How could this happen to me? Nothing was more important to me than upholding the image of a successful Asian marriage. Nothing was more important than my desire to uphold the Asian honor of a good marriage. The cultural shame was compounded by religious shame. I belonged to an Asian-American church at the time. Everything that I believed in about a Christian marriage had disintegrated in front of me.

I felt like a failure not just to myself but to my immediate family, grandparents, deceased ancestors, church, and the Asian community at large. The double stigma within my culture of divorce and addiction haunted me. How had this happened? How could I be so weak? God must hate me.

## You're Fired!

At the same time as my divorce proceedings, Terry continued to harangue me and I questioned if I would get a contract renewal. I couldn't take it anymore and snapped. Since my marriage was a lost cause, I confronted Terry and asked if I had a future with the company. He wouldn't say one way or another, but hinted there were hundreds of people ready to take my place.

Since he wasn't willing to give me an answer, I told him I would file a complaint for what he did to me during my interview nearly two years prior. He stared back unfazed and responded, "Sam, I don't know what you're talking about." I reminded him that he got me drunk and tried to have sex with me, but he remained steadfast in his belief that nothing egregious had occurred. I revealed to him that I had a recording of the phone conversation and would turn it into human resources to help refresh his memory. With this bombshell, his face turned pale and he calmly uttered, "Sam, I don't think that's a good idea." But I had made up my mind. I wasn't going down without a fight and I called HR the next day.

I had no lawyer, financial resources, or understanding of HR and thought the department was my friend. The woman from HR seemed very interested in my concerns and asked if I could come in and talk to her about them. I transcribed the entire recorded phone conversation I had with Terry during that time and gave it to her. Shortly afterwards, she asked if I could hand her the tape so she could listen to it. It was my only copy and after I shared this information with my therapist he suggested I find an attorney. I quickly found one and she instructed me to keep the tape in a safe place and to not give it to HR under any circumstances. The tone from HR changed immediately. I was scared and confused, as they were so nice prior to the attorney stepping in. HR informed me to stay home and not return to work until told otherwise. For nearly three weeks, coworkers wondered why I wasn't working and I told them I was struggling with depression from my divorce. No one knew the true reason. When I returned, Terry was not in the office and no one knew why. I started to worry that others in the newsroom would realize it was related to me.

Finally, my attorney called and said, "Congratulations, Sam. You did it. You got him fired. You should feel proud, as this rarely happens." Technically, Terry was forced to resign and I was to do the same. I agreed to a severance package worth $20,000, as I was desperate to pay off mounting legal fees to this attorney and my divorce lawyer. While I netted no profit from the situation, I did gain an understanding of how sexual assault perpetrators like Terry groom victims and use that power and leverage to get what they want, often with few repercussions.

## Help Is a Four-letter Word

Asking for help is hard enough. But in the Asian world, it's considered a four-letter word. It's obscene. It's taboo. Now add in the complexity and shame of an addiction and you have the making of a cultural curse. I fought against it at many points along the way. I detested help. I was caught in a bind because my recovery was dependent on reaching out to others for help, yet acknowledging an addiction would be considered a curse to my family and the wider culture. Asian addicts either go against the grain of their culture and risk ostracism or suffer in silence and succumb to long-term, debilitating bouts of depression, anxiety, suicide, and feelings of inadequacy. I was willing to risk the ostracism, as I felt I had hit "rock bottom."

My cycle of sexual shame and addiction had reached a breaking point. Despite the appearances of professional success as an on-air television reporter in Los Angeles, my world was unraveling. I was suffering from depression and unemployment and through a divorce. Sara and I had attended an Asian-American Christian church where the pastor recommended therapy for me. He was the only person outside of family who knew my situation. Since I held him in high esteem, I took his advice and found a therapist. The therapist wasted no time in exploring my immigrant Chinese background, where we uncovered the generational standard of emotional stoicism.

## Asians Don't Cry

My parents had been programmed to unquestionably subscribe to the cultural values of harmony and collectivism. Emotionally, I was discouraged from showing any weakness and I was told that strength and a strong will would prevail. I don't recall ever having a conversation or being able to tell my parents when I felt anxious, scared, confused, angry, disappointed, or hurt. It was unconsciously ingrained in me that it was not permissible to hurt. When I did hurt, I buried those feelings. In therapy, I knew it was socially acceptable to grieve the loss of a marriage, yet the armor of suppressing these feelings was strong, as noted in my journal entries:

> I really wish I knew what my heart is feeling right now. It's so protected, I won't let anyone near it, including myself. (February 2003)

Therapy was working and in a few short weeks the safety of being real with another human being gave me permission to cry:

> The past few days have been quite a breakthrough. I'm beginning to allow my emotions and sadness to come out. In therapy I used four Kleenexes! Very sad about losing Sara and my mother-in-

*law. I feel so lonely. They were the two people in the whole world I felt most connected to.* (March 2003)

Dr. Steve was the psychologist referred to me from a friend at church. He was not only a practicing therapist but he taught psychology at Fuller Seminary in Pasadena. I saw him every week during the late mornings and I began looking forward to the sessions. He was very inquisitive, unlike what the Freud caricatures I saw depicted, where the clients do all the talking and the therapist is half-asleep. He asked about my childhood, my relationships with my family, the impact of racism growing up, my peer network, my support group, and myriad other aspects of life that I initially thought was a waste of time: Why are we talking about my family when I have a porn/sex problem? But it started making sense as early as a few weeks into therapy. The big themes related to attachment ruptures, racism, immigration and acculturation, abandonment trauma, and childhood neglect became all too apparent once he began to provide the psycho-education around these issues and how they can impact one's ability to cope through life.

Soon I was not only grieving the loss of my marriage but the unspoken disappointments of childhood in an Asian home. Some of those childhood wounds tapped into the deep grief of not having parents available to me physically or emotionally. I had questioned what masculinity meant for me. In an Asian culture in which boys are shamed for having emotions, what was I to do with my emotions? Is it "manly" to have them?

*I'm feeling the pain of not having Dad close to me and how hurt and fragile I am, even to this day. I am sad for him, as well that grandpa didn't learn how to love his kids. I am now finally entering the grief stage.* (March 2003)

I also struggled with the wider concept of unconditional love from my parents. In our family, the message repeated by our parents was to "get good grades, get a good job, get married, and have kids." I never felt they understood my heart's desires. There was limited attunement to my hopes, dreams, and aspirations. I wanted my parents to ask about my school day, my favorite subjects, and my extracurricular interests. Instead, they operated with a hands-off approach to parenting that eventually left me with a gnawing sense of emptiness. I believed I was not worth much in their eyes.

> *I am starting to see how desperately I've looked my whole life to find value in myself, value in my work to make me feel good about myself. That can't go on any longer. Sure, I can have big dreams and go after success, but I can't hope that success will fill me spiritually and emotionally. I need to love myself right now for who I am, stripped of all things I've had that made me feel good: a job, a wife, money, etc. I am a worthy person. A God-given gift to the world. I need to believe that!* (April 2003)

## Love Is Unnecessary

Chinese culture relies heavily on not expressing love through words. To this day many Chinese believe that telling your children you love them has the potential to coddle them and make them emotionally indulgent. It's discouraged to emotionally or physically affirm children with hugs, kisses, or "good job" or "I love you." This lack of physical and verbal affirmation in childhood was one of the key learning moments for me in the therapeutic process. Without physical affirmation, serious relational ruptures can occur. Children crave touch. They crave the opportunity to be held closely by their parents. Touch helps children feel safe, loved, and secure.

The one moment in my childhood where touch occurred was when my mother would pick my earwax using a Chinese instrument made of metal. I cherished every minute of having my ear on her lap. When she was finished, I would always tell her to keep looking. I knew there wasn't more wax to be excavated, but I yearned for a few more precious moments of having one side of my face resting on her lap. Years later my mother told me, "We love from our heart and that's what counts!"

In therapy, I learned to understand how the lack of physical and emotional affirmation made me vulnerable to desiring it from other women and, if they weren't available, through the fantasy of porn. Eventually, as my emotions began to stabilize, Dr. Steve suggested group therapy for me.

I reacted negatively to this idea, telling him, "I don't want to join a group of 'losers.'" I believed I was better than others who struggled with porn. I was educated, a working professional, and "normal." I couldn't envision sitting in a room with other guys who I viewed as perverted, weirdos, and societal degenerates. I bristled at the idea of associating myself with a group of "sex addicts," but finally relented.

I can still vividly recall that first day of group therapy. There was a sense of dread in the hours leading up to it. I was ten minutes late due to traffic and, once I approached the door to the office, I paused, hesitated, and considered turning around and leaving. But once I heard voices on the other side, I took a deep breath, knocked on the door, and entered into a room with six other men who eagerly got up from their seats to shake my hand and introduce themselves.

In the blink of an eye, I had a paradigm shift. The guys looked "normal." Each group member looked like an "average Joe." They were dressed in semi-casual clothes, were of average build, and had professional jobs. Many were married and had children. This was not what I was expecting. I had imagined ghoulish and dark personalities who didn't know how to interact with women and just wanted to hide in a corner. The normality of everyone around me shattered my perceptions of what a sex addict looked like.

The attitude of the men in the group also struck me. Despite many of them going through a divorce, there was a collective enthusiasm in their tone of voice and facial expressions. They looked like they enjoyed being with each other. After I took my seat, the therapist suggested I just listen as the others introduced themselves and explained why they were in therapy. As each person shared his story a bond began to form, as I heard, for the first time, similarities to my own story. The therapist then asked me to share whatever I felt comfortable with. I dove right in and told them I was going through a divorce and that I had struggled with sexual escapism as early as eight years old, which escalated to sex and then porn in my young adult life. To share my story and have them validate it was one of the most cathartic experiences of my life. Up until that point, I had not met a soul who also struggled with porn/sex as an addictive behavior. The men also encouraged me to read books on addictions and relationships and join them at their weekly dinners prior to the group sessions.

One of the group members was part Filipino. It was hard to tell Jeff was Asian until he told me, as I thought he was possibly Hispanic. Still, it was a cultural connection that added to my sense of belonging. He asked me if I would like to go to the gym with him during the days we had group therapy, as another means to bond, and since I liked working out I accepted his invitation.

Thursdays became my full day of self-care. I would drive from Los Angeles to Orange County to work out with Jeff, eat dinner with the group, and attend group therapy, before making the hour drive back home to Los Angeles.

Since healthy attachment did not occur in childhood, I was learning it for the first time with these guys. I could finally express my deepest and darkest thoughts and feelings without fear of judgment. Thoughts and insecurities that have followed me through life were now being verbalized and heard. I shared about my role as the oldest son to a first-generation Chinese immigrant family and how so much had been placed on my shoulders. It was a heavy burden to succeed in ways that no one else in my family had. The men in the group seemed to agree that my compulsive sexual behaviors were tied to societal stereotypes and pressures. They also helped explain why I gravitated toward sexual escapism. There was a lack of maternal nurturing, to be sure, but racism and anti-Asian male masculinity also had me fixated on proving to myself and the world that Asian men were sexual. Additionally, the men helped me break down the wall to my own lack of sensitivity. My emotions had been hardened through life—and through Chinese cultural programming generations prior.

My upbringing of stoicism and Asian honor was noticeable from their perspective. They'd give me direct feedback when they saw my "Asian shame" rearing its ugly head. During one meeting, when I was sharing about a particularly hard week, I relayed my challenges by trying to portray an upbeat demeanor. The guys quickly saw the emotional disconnect and challenged me. "Sam, why are you smiling and trying to put on a positive image when your life is blowing up?" I responded, "Because I'm Asian and I was taught not to dwell on the negative!" Prior to this, I had viewed the men as weak when they would cry or share about their sadness. However, over the course of the next year, I had a number of breakthroughs, as we processed my family's challenges as new immigrants to this country and the impact it had on me. My ability to be emotionally vulnerable, honest, and transparent was growing. Never had I opened up to others and received not only validation but feedback that challenged my way of thinking. We had permission to call each other out on our denials, minimizations, and other distorted ways of thinking.

Another aspect that was revealed to me was my family role as the "hero." In group therapy, the roles were shared, explained, and each of us was given permission to take on a new role. Instead of seeing myself as the hero who had to be perfect, I could ask this hero part to take the role of being real and authentic. I didn't have to have a cheerful, smiling façade that refused to admit fear. Instead, I could finally just be me. The pain, hurt, and feelings of abandonment erupted from the deepest cavity of my heart. I no longer had to put on a fake exterior of being upbeat, entertaining, or fun. The facade I had worked so hard to develop in childhood was being transformed into an authentic self.

Despite periods of epiphany, the process of growth was not always linear and positive. There were many moments of doubt and despair and many setbacks.

## From Red Carpet Events to Homeless Camps

After nearly a year and a half of individual and group therapy, it was time to look for work. The NBC station in Portland was hiring and I was offered and immediately accepted the job, since it would put me within a three-hour drive from Seattle. Lots of stories in Portland focused on homelessness. This was much different from doing red-carpet events interviewing movie stars and other celebrity-driven news events. The job quickly lost its luster after a month of standing in the rain doing live reports. But I went through the motions, as this was the only work I knew how to do.

The work pressure was there, but coming from a different perspective. The question was not if I could do well coming from a smaller market, but if I could live up to the hype and expectations of a big-city reporter coming from Los Angeles. I didn't have the safety and accountability of my past therapists and group members and was feeling alone having to start over once again. I began looking at pornography and tried to find sexual partners while on the job. When I interviewed people for news stories, I tried to assess if the women were open to relationships or just a fling. It might be a flirtatious comment or even a seemingly innocuous follow-up meeting for coffee to see if they might be game for pleasure instead of business.

One woman I had a brief interlude with was older but single. I could tell she was willing to be sexual based on her banter with me. When we'd go out for coffee, she'd joke and flirt with me by stroking my arm and asking me if I wanted to go back to her place. Since she was a brunette, I obviously didn't put up much resistance.

# Bali, Indonesia |

Being in the news business, I had covered enough stories in which unsuspecting men would get arrested for soliciting prostitutes and get caught on camera. I was determined not to jeopardize my career, so instead I chose to visit prostitutes only overseas. When I occasionally travelled abroad, I felt justified, knowing that it was legal or at the very least tolerated by the local governments in Europe and parts of Asia.

In 2005, I was in Bali, Indonesia for my brother's wedding. Bali was known for its deep-tissue massages, so one night I went and paid for a massage. Afterwards, I got into the taxi and was planning to go back to my hotel when the driver asked if I wanted to "have some fun" that night. He winked at me, and I was pretty sure that was code for something sexual. He drove nearly thirty minutes, out into the country. He pointed to an apartment-like structure and motioned me to go toward the building and he'd wait for me until I was done. The building looked like a nondescript motel without any signage.

Approaching the building, I was greeted by a Balinese man who spoke broken English. He asked me if I was American, and when I said "yes" he led me down a dirt path that ended at a glass window with three dozen women on the other side sitting in rows of clay or dirt. It was reminiscent of a zoo; I was the paying customer and the women were the entertainment to be looked at. They were wearing bathing suits and had a small number pinned to their waist. The man in charge asked me which one I liked and, after some furtive glances at the forlorn faces, I chose a Balinese woman who looked the most European to me in terms of facial features. Minutes later, the woman I had selected was put in a room and I was asked to go in. I, of course, assumed she was a prostitute and this was how things worked in Bali. I paid her fifty dollars and we had sex. She spoke limited English and I tried to assuage my guilt by smiling a lot and hoping she'd view me as a "nice" guy. But in the end, it was transactional, and there's no denying that. I felt something was off, but was unsure what it was. The entire experience felt dark and sinister. The women didn't seem to have any choice and appeared to be held captive. They took directions from the men who were there. They never talked back or disagreed. They simply listened and complied.

I didn't think much more about it until years later, when sex trafficking became known to the general population through popular culture and outreach efforts. One outreach took place on a Sunday morning during the announcement period prior to the main service at my church. Christian humanitarian workers came in and educated the congregation about the sex-trade industry in Asia, while requesting prayers for and financial contributions to the agency they worked for, which helped women who have escaped trafficking with shelter, counseling, and life skills. They ticked off some of the countries impacted by sex trafficking, including Vietnam, Thailand, and Indonesia. My heart skipped a beat as I made the connection to my own experience in Bali and the strong possibility it was part of a sex-trafficking ring. I believe the women I saw that night were taken from their families, thinking they were going to work in a legitimate business, only to be trapped in a life of endless sexual trauma and despair. The pit of my stomach still can't fathom how far down my addiction had taken me.

*Sam with his on-air colleagues in Missoula, Montana, 1995*

*Sam and his colleagues from Toledo, Ohio, 1997*

*Sam in a cornfield in Toledo, Ohio, 1998*

# Part III

# The Wounded Healer

## Los Angeles Revisited

After nearly two years of working in Portland, I wanted out and started looking for other journalism jobs. As luck would have it, the PBS station in Los Angeles was searching for a reporter to do long-format stories up to six minutes in length. No live reporting was required and I could spend a week working on a segment, compared to the short daily, local news stories I was accustomed to. The downside was the lack of job security. All my other jobs came with a contract. This one was dependent on funding. If the show lost funding, I'd be out of a job, but the news director reassured me staff would get at least three months's notice if that ever occurred. That was enough for me to accept the job on the spot.

The work was great. I had the opportunity to slow down and spend quality time producing stories. I pitched a number of pieces related to mental health, addiction, and psychotherapy during my first two years there. With such a keen interest in this field, my colleagues suggested I consider going into it. I brushed it aside, thinking I could never go back to school since I didn't consider myself a good student. All of this changed when I was accepted into a two-week journalism fellowship in South Korea. This gave me a chance to take a break from my PBS gig while getting paid to travel to South Korea and learn.

During the fellowship, I was surrounded by a handful of top-notch journalists. One woman was an anchor for CNN. There were columnists from *USA Today* and the *Seattle Times*. I felt like an imposter, as my main interest in going to South Korea was to eat tasty food and enjoy the sights and sounds like a tourist. Our daytime activities consisted of meetings and workshops with diplomats, politicians, and other high-ranking government officials. While the conversations centered on geo-political issues, my mind started daydreaming of how I could better spend my time. I wondered what it would be like to swap out this environment for one focused on therapy.

Over the course of my time in South Korea, I had many opportunities to get to know the other journalists when our official day ended and we would go out and enjoy the nightlife. During one of these conversations someone brought up the topic of relationships and I offered some advice that was well-received. One of the journalists asked if I read books on this matter and I told her I have a library full of books related to counseling and relationships. When the others heard this, they all gathered around me and shared how they could tell this was a genuine passion of mine and encouraged me to seriously explore working in the field of counseling. I quickly responded that I'm not a good student or gave some excuse as to why I couldn't do it. They wouldn't accept my response and persisted in helping me see that I had a real interest in the field. I had not seriously entertained this idea. I was enjoying my work at the PBS station. I could finally just write and report without the fear of stumbling over myself on live television. I had also developed a groove, having worked there for nearly two years, so I didn't want to disrupt that with the challenges of graduate school. Nevertheless, the feedback from these colleagues left an impact on me.

In a moment of surrender on the return flight to Los Angeles, I remember praying to God. I closed my eyes and asked if He really wanted me to leave a comfortable career. If so, I asked that he open doors to graduate school and make it unequivocally known that this was the next chapter in my life.

I applied to a handful of graduate schools in Southern California that offered evening classes so I could continue working. I was accepted at Azusa Pacific University, which was thirty miles east of where I was living in South Pasadena. It seemed like my prayer had been answered. Not only was I going to start an evening program, my boss at the PBS station was equally excited and flexed my schedule so I could leave a bit early on the two nights when I had classes.

Graduate school was an amazing experience. I got to soak in the information offered in the classes related to family systems and cultural issues. I was pursuing a master's degree in clinical psychology with an emphasis in marriage and family therapy. Consequently, I was also required to undergo at least one year of therapy while in grad school. I found Nicole, a therapist close to my apartment in Pasadena, and had weekly sessions with her for three years.

Working with Nicole brought out different issues. Since she was a woman, specific issues of female rejection or my perceived fears of rejection became more prominent in sessions. It also gave me a new understanding of what healthy emotional intimacy with a woman could look like, as I was learning to relate to a woman beyond my old superficial self. Unlike with Dr. Steve, I was hesitant to open up about my pornography and sexual issues with Nicole. Even though she was a therapist, she was a female first. The thought of her recoiling in horror was my big fear, so I waited a couple of months before I shared that information. During the first few sessions, I would share bits and pieces of my shameful past and watch to see her reaction. If she didn't physically or verbally judge me, I felt safe enough to share more, eventually letting her know the full reason why I wanted therapy beyond the pat answer of "therapy is required as part of my graduate school." To my surprise, when I divulged that I had been addicted to porn for years, she didn't show any signs of disgust or condemnation. She was curious about my behaviors, how it started, and what I was getting in return. Her response brought additional healing to my shame of wanting to hide this part of myself from women. I was learning to accept my past because others like Nicole were accepting of me. Acceptance, though, didn't mean she endorsed what I did. She simply challenged me to think about the women in porn as real people to deter my behaviors. This was tremendously helpful because when I'm triggered to look at porn, I think of the women as daughters, mothers, and sisters with real lives and families versus my past way of viewing them simply as objects for my own needs. With regards to the prostitutes, she offered that many of those women come from trauma and abuse and wasn't hesitant to tell me that my actions fuel an industry that capitalizes on female trauma. This was another eye-opening revelation, as I had justified that the prostitutes were making their own free choice to engage in their behaviors for profit. Nicole stated that women in those situations usually don't have much choice because unresolved trauma functions as a means to steer them into a cycle of more abuse and trauma, even if they are making money from it. It was like throwing cold water on my face; for so long I played the victim, and this new perspective gave me additional tools to realize I can make different choices in terms of finding emotional refuge elsewhere.

Even though Nicole was white, she was comfortable exploring my Chinese heritage and how it affected me. She wasn't afraid to let me know that, regardless of ethnicity, children need a certain amount of physical and emotional nurturing to feel safe and secure. I still struggled to acknowledge that I didn't get enough from my parents and told her, like I did Dr. Steve, that I felt like I was blaming my parents for my behavior. But because Nicole was a mother, she used anecdotes related to her parenting style and periodically asked if my "child" self could see what it wanted back then. Her shift in asking me to look at my childhood from my child's eye gave me a new perspective not just on the pain I endured but it disabled the protective part of me that resisted associating negativity with my parents. By doing so I was able to realize that my immigrant parents did do the best they could, but that my younger self desperately craved and needed more. It was okay to cry for the little boy in me who didn't get nurtured the way he wanted, while also seeing his parents as loving. My parents could love me only to the extent they were loved as children and to the extent the Chinese culture they learned in Hong Kong would allow. This was a powerful moment in my healing.

But like with any relationship, Nicole and I had some obstacles. When I saw her get out of her Volvo SUV, I rolled my eyes. I told her that despite our progress she couldn't truly understand me. When she inquired what that meant, I responded, "How can a white female therapist like you, living a suburban life and driving a Volvo SUV, possibly relate to a Chinese immigrant who grew up in poverty among African-Americans?" She opened up and disclosed that she was married to a Black singer and knew all the R&B songs I had referenced in our sessions. She also shared that she grew up in a lower, middle-class neighborhood in New Jersey among different ethnic groups and conceded that, while she couldn't totally understand my situation, she could relate to my circumstances. Her answer was enough for me.

Ironically, in my three years working with Nicole, one the most impactful and healing things she did for me was not in session but outside the office. She knew I was looking for internships and mentioned she'd put in a good word for me at a couple of clinics I had applied to. I was floored. I knew she cared for me, but for her to put her name on the line for me was incomprehensible. I tried to hold back the tears, but she noticed them and asked me, "If your tears could talk, what would they say?" I told her, "My tears can't believe you find me worthy enough to vouch for as a person." There were five minutes left in the session, no more words were exchanged. Words weren't needed. Her validation touched a deep part of me that felt I wasn't good enough for her validation. I spent the remaining minutes just thanking her with my eyes.

## 'God Loves My Divorce'

When I got divorced in 2001, I knew of just one other Asian friend who had gone through a divorce. That is how shameful divorce is in the Asian community. Asians would prefer to stay married for the sake of the family rather than get divorced and risk social ostracism. I've known people whose parents slept in separate rooms and ignored each other, yet stayed legally married. Or on the other extreme, the Asian parents got divorced but still lived together for the sake of honor.

After my divorce, when I went on dates, I felt I had to be honest about my marital status. I've heard stories about women getting married, only to find out later their husbands had been previously married.

I wasn't willing to lie about my marital status, but I did notice a shift once I mentioned I was divorced. Some of the religious Asian women would interrogate me about how my faith and divorce could coincide or align. They'd ask questions such as, "Sam, how do you think God views your divorce?" I would respond in a deadpan voice, "God loves my divorce!"

After a few dates, during which I initially dreaded disclosing my divorce, I changed strategies and disclosed it at the first opportunity. It was empowering because I was no longer tiptoeing around such a vital part of my life experience but went on the offensive. If women had a problem with it, I knew from the start it wasn't meant to be.

## 'Divorce Recovery Coach'

Since I was still in graduate school, I couldn't work as a therapist, but there's no law in the U.S. to stop anyone from calling themselves a "life coach." So I had some business cards made and even bought rooftop signage for my car and labeled myself a "divorce recovery coach."

It was bold and brash and my cohorts in graduate school were impressed by my hustle and chutzpah. Everywhere I went, I told people what I was doing. The downtown Los Angeles YMCA staff even allowed me to use their offices and offer free life-coaching sessions to members. Some of those sessions parlayed into paid sessions.

When I wasn't hustling or studying, I played basketball. When one of my basketball buddies realized I was in school for counseling, he suggested introducing me to a friend of his who was already working as a therapist. I didn't know he was also Asian-American, so when we met it was like meeting a long, lost brother.

## My Soul Mate Is a Man?

John Kim is a Korean-American therapist who goes by the moniker "The Angry Therapist." He was an Asian therapist who was not only divorced but went public with it. He would post blogs about his status as a divorced and angry man who came from a stereotypical immigrant Korean household devoid of emotions, except shame and scorn. We connected quickly because of our backgrounds. Not only were we two Asian-American divorced men, we came from a writing background. John was once a Hollywood screenwriter, albeit, he admitted, a miserable, detached, and angry one, due to his feelings of inadequacy in generating any money from it.

We moved in together and lived in Los Angeles's Koreatown while I started my career in counseling. Part of our desire was to live differently and boldly. We agreed to get rid of our televisions and spend our free time hanging out together. Instead of watching TV, we'd go to coffee shops and talk, read, and meet other people for conversation. We craved emotional intimacy both with each other and with those courageous enough to join us.

During John's work hours, he would blog and post videos of himself sharing stories of his anger, depression, divorce, and a host of other emotional maladies for all to see. I was encouraged, awed, and moved by his rawness while finishing up my last year of grad school. We both acknowledged our lives were forever changed by our divorce and rebirth. We no longer hid in shame but encouraged each other to share our stories with others as our new calling. He is what I'd consider my soul mate, not in the conventional, romantic sense but because of our deep bond and the understanding we have of each other.

Our time living together would be brief, as, upon graduation, I received an offer to work in Hong Kong to help a church launch its counseling department. I accepted the offer and decided to return home to Seattle and enjoy the summer and reconnect with friends before moving to Hong Kong. In the midst of my time at home, I was notified that the position would be put on hold indefinitely. What was I to do now with no job?

## Boomerang Kid

"Boomerang Kids" is a term used to describe adult children who return to their parents's home due to financial issues, usually shortly after college. In a way I was just a much older boomerang kid. I was thirty-five years old, living in my parents's basement with a promising job offer rescinded. I had my master's degree displayed prominently on my desk, but it did little to prop up my sense of inadequacy. Despite my academic accomplishment, I was embarrassed by my dependency on my parents. It was hard, as I valued autonomy, independence, and separation from my parents when I left for college nearly twenty years earlier. Now I had boomeranged back into their house.

I had the downstairs to myself, but it was still challenging. I heard Chinese soap operas blaring loudly all hours of the day. They numbed out on television and by going to the casino. Vestiges of the past came forth again, as I felt very alone in this household. My dad uttered short phrases that sounded pre-programmed: "Good morning, Sam" and "It's going to be cold today, so make sure to wear a jacket." When I ate with them I assumed the role of dutiful son by politely nodding whenever they spoke generic Chinese platitudes: "Don't shake your legs or you'll shake away your future good fortunes" and "No matter how big, one beam cannot support a house." That last proverb was my parents's reminder, lest I forget, that Chinese collectivist thinking about the group first is still to be cherished above the Western values of autonomy and independence.

Troubled by the lack of connection at home, I looked to my growing community for support. I began playing basketball with childhood friends, met new friends through counseling network events, and started attending Asian-American churches in the area. I was determined not to let this old environment bring back old thoughts and habits.

## Asian Teen Outreach

After making six figures toward the end of my broadcast-journalism career, I had a rude awakening in the counseling realm. My first job out of graduate school was working as a school outreach counselor at an Asian Counseling Clinic close to my parents's house. The salary was $35,000 a year. The clinic focused its work on Asian refugees and immigrants as well as their Americanized children. South Seattle was growing and the clinic reflected the diversity. Beyond Asian therapists who spoke numerous languages, there was also a number of East African counselors to help the newer immigrants from Eritrea, Ethiopia, Somalia, and Kenya.

I was paired with a Chinese therapist who was born in Singapore, spent her formative childhood in South Africa, and spoke with a British accent. That was very confusing for the urban Asian kids and they didn't know what to make of her. She would also use metric terms like kilometers (instead of miles) and ask where the "loo" was. She often shared how her unique background made her feel like a unicorn. Wherever she went, she'd say acceptance was hard to find. She was South African by nationality, Chinese by ethnicity, yet Singaporean culturally. I thought I had identity issues being a Chinese guy born in Hong Kong (under British Rule) who thought I was "Black on the inside." Despite our vast cultural differences, she and I could commiserate that people in America too often pigeonhole us and neglect to recognize how nuanced and challenging our lives can be because of our mixed identities.

Our work at the clinic was outreach to elementary and middle school students as a means for them to build healthy relationships. It was psycho-education and more prevention-based compared to traditional therapy, where students came in to see counselors for their issues. Still, it was a good experience because we learned ways of building trust through games and other social activities, which allowed the kids to open up to us about their stressors.

## Black-on-White Racism

Because our work was in the Seattle Public School district, the students were primarily ethnic minorities of Black, Asian, and East African descent. Racism in childhood often rears its ugly head in school cafeterias, on playgrounds, and in other places where teachers and staff don't have the eyes and ears to catch it. This was no different in our after-school program.

One eventful afternoon, I blew the whistle to signal the end of a dodgeball game. Out of the corner of my eye, I saw several elementary school Black students throw their balls directly at the face of a white student on the opposing team. His face became flushed and he cried profusely, accusing the kids of picking on him. It's hard to say if this incident was racism, but since he and his sister were the only white kids in the program, I kept that in consideration.

In America, we tend to consider the possibility of racism only if an incident was blatantly racist. If no words were used to suggest racism, our judicial system is hamstrung. But ethnic minorities know racism includes more than direct, overt, or explicit behaviors or words. In this dodgeball incident, when I saw the Black students targeting the lone white student, I intervened and asked what happened. The Black students were in denial and said they didn't do it. I responded, "Hey, kids. Don't play dumb. I saw it with my own eyes." I followed up by giving them a stern warning that picking on another student who "looked different" from them was not allowed in our program. The next thing I knew, the parents had complained that I had mistreated their children in a demeaning and racist manner. Apparently, the students concocted a narrative that I had called them "stupid Black kids."

The parents wanted me removed from the program. My supervisor asked if she could reassign me to another school as a means to appease the parents. I stood my ground and told her I, in good conscience, couldn't do that, as it felt like an admission of guilt. In the end, I resigned. It was quite a drastic turn of events, but I learned something about race I wasn't aware of until that experience. Issues of race can be distorted to fit the narrative of whoever has the most power to influence the outcome. In my case, it came from the Black kids and their parents, whereas in mainstream society, the white establishment and institutions typically wield the power.

Once again, I was out of a job, and my parents heaped shame on me. In Chinese there's a phrase for when you get fired—chǎo yóuyú—which translated means "fried squid." They would ask me why I was fried squid. I couldn't explain the complexities of office politics to them and they reasoned I had become too stubborn because of my American education.

Fortunately, there's a demand for counselors. I quickly found two jobs: one during the day as a school counselor and the other at night at a psychiatric clinic. While working and living with my parents, I was able to pay off my sizeable student-loan debt. Since I was working two jobs, I was also quickly accruing hours toward full licensure as a therapist, which would mean no more mandatory supervision.

For the school counselor position, I was stationed at an alternative high school for students who, for a variety of reasons, couldn't thrive at public schools. I was told to be creative and think "out of the box," as these students wouldn't respond well to sit-down therapy. I learned an invaluable lesson here: When working with kids, find things they like and participate with them. I played basketball with the students, helped them cook (there were cooking classes), and dedicated time to artwork and games like chess. It helped to quickly build trust. They saw I could be flexible and open-minded. I was also self-deprecating, in order to let them know I didn't take life too seriously.

Additionally, I worked the graveyard shift at a downtown Seattle psychiatric clinic. My responsibility at the clinic was to ensure the residents were safe and accounted for when they turned in for the night. Occasionally some of them wanted a smoke break and I hit a button that allowed them in and out of the security gate. The residents suffered severe psychiatric issues, including schizophrenia, delusions, and paranoia. One resident kept calling me "Yul Brynner" because, since I was bald, I reminded him of the late actor.

The clinic was hard on the senses. The foul stench of dried urine permeated the two floors I was overseeing. Some of residents reeked of body odor because they had not showered in weeks. A couple of the residents had the unfortunate compulsion to throw feces at the walls and thought the feces was paint to create their Picassos with. I retched more than I care to remember. While cleaning wasn't part of the job description, I spent many evenings mopping the floors with a bucket full of water and bleach.

My other main function at the clinic was dispensing medications. Each client had a predetermined cup of medication and I gave them out in the morning after breakfast. I was flabbergasted by how medicated they were. Some clients took more than ten different psychotropic pills at one time (and they would get the same dosage after lunch and dinner).

## Eating Disorders

After stints working with youth and psychiatric patients, I realized those populations weren't my calling. I wanted to work with functional adults and incorporate my knowledge of addiction or help ethnic minorities dealing with acculturation issues like the ones I went through. I went to a job fair at an eating disorder clinic and the clinic had openings for therapists. I was hired and was finally working with clients with issues related to addiction. This was so different from the psychiatric population. The clinic was immaculate and artistic. I enjoyed just looking at the art on the walls. However, working with clients who are forced to attend treatment provided quite the challenge.

My job was to eat with them, monitor their behaviors, and encourage them to finish their meals. I was in charge of estimating the percentage of how much each patient ate during a meal. The percentage was a measurement of a client's progress, so the higher the number, the better off they were considered in terms of nutritional health and recovery. In my time there I saw a trend. Adoptees, sexual abuse victims, and those with alcohol or drug addiction were more vulnerable to eating disorders. The common denominator was trauma. Whether the clients were aware of how it impacted their eating behaviors was another story. The intensity of an inpatient facility was eventually too much for me. The clients just weren't physically or mentally able to do more in-depth therapy, due to being so malnourished. My bosses told me to avoid the clients' trauma and just do superficial work, such as helping them regulate themselves with ice when they got nervous or calming them down with deep breathing. I could do only so many mindfulness exercises before my head exploded, but the overall experience did light a fire in me to continue down the road of trauma and addiction work.

## Sex Addicts and Offenders

In my hunt for more addiction work, I came across a job posting at a private group that specialized in sex addiction and court-mandated sex-offender treatment. Given my background, this was intriguing and I wanted to learn more about how to work with clients dealing with problematic sexual behaviors.

During this time working for the private group, I would run up to four meetings a week with porn/sex addicts, as well as the court-mandated sex-offender clientele. The work was gratifying and communal; we'd have weekly staff meetings to talk about our cases. I also got instant, informal feedback from coworkers in between client meetings and during my lunch breaks. However, most of the clients were older white men who matched the demographic of the owner of the practice, Dr. Bill. After a couple of years working for the psychologist I had earned my hours toward full licensure and wanted to make a mark in the field by catering to more ethnic clients, and I decided to hang my shingle as a therapist with my own private practice.

## On My Own

I called every sex-addiction therapist I could find in the Seattle area, so I could meet them in person and introduce myself to them. One psychologist who worked with sex offenders and sex addicts related to my desire to work with ethnic clients, as she was part Hispanic and part Japanese. Dr. Myrna Pinedo became a mentor of sorts to me, giving me advice and copies of all the intake forms she used and suggesting I tweak the forms to fit my practice. She even let me sublet an office from her on a daily and even hourly basis, depending on my needs. The office had a small sofa and a therapist chair, along with a large storage bin that served as a file cabinet.

It was thrilling to finally be on my own. My success or my failure was dependent on me alone, just like other small business owners. I did all the requisite work of establishing a business license, getting insurance, and putting up my profile on various counseling-referral websites. I began writing a blog for *Psychology Today*. Due to my blog, collegial references, and my name in the community, clients began trickling in.

Some of my first blog entries were related to Asian cultural shame and addiction. Even though it seemed repetitive, I told myself to keep writing about this topic, as the number of viewer clicks indicated there was interest in it. Since I didn't have many clients early on, I did a lot of reading and writing. I went to networking events, and other therapists kept reminding me of how much I was needed in this field, as a minority for like-minded clients to relate to. My blogs began to gain traction and I got noticed to the point where local counseling agencies and university psychology programs would ask me to come in and present on this topic. That was validating. My content was desired among those in the field. But others outside of the field also took notice. I was invited to speak at libraries and colleges related to the "Asian-American Experience." At first, the presentations were pro bono, but I enjoyed them. Crafting the power-point slides and fine-tuning my delivery, punctuated with spoken-word poetry, became a form of artistic expression. The presentations gave me opportunities to do outreach in this area, which I felt was vital. I wanted to encourage others to seek counseling and to validate the struggles of ethnic minorities, especially immigrants or those struggling with addictions. In other words, embedded within the presentations were glimpses of my own life story. They weren't focused on me per se, but I did reveal enough of myself so others in the audience wouldn't feel ashamed of their own experiences or desire to ask for help.

When clients came into my office, I asked them why they chose me. They said they wanted an Asian-American therapist who understood the dynamics of growing up with traditional Asian parents. For those dealing with addictions, I was able to give them the grace they needed by providing a space where they could share their inner thoughts and demons without any fear of judgment.

While some clients have read my books or blogs and know of my addiction history, the majority of them do not know about it. In therapy this is called self-disclosure. Some addiction therapists openly share their history on their websites and in their introductions with clients to build a bond and connection. I tend to be a bit more judicious, but will share my past if I feel it's warranted. For example, if I get a sense a client thinks I have it all together and can't relate to his or her divorce or separation, I open up and tell them I've gone through a divorce as well. I don't go into details, but I share just enough so they will realize I'm not immune to human pain and suffering. I will also open up if a client is struggling with porn/sex addiction and thinks I can't understand the challenges of recovery.

My private practice is a dream come true. I have the balance I've always wanted in terms of client ethnic diversity and the myriad issues coming in. In one of my sex-addiction groups, there are more ethnic minorities than white clients. It's gratifying to see Asian and other ethnic clients taking the courageous steps toward getting help.

Nevertheless, due to the atypical nature of my work, I still get reminded by some Asian friends that I don't have a regular job with regular hours. (A full practice is twenty client hours per week.) This is not said in a warm and encouraging way, but more as a slight that I'm not really working as hard as I should or could. Initially, I felt a twinge of inadequacy and thought maybe they are right. Maybe I should ditch my private practice and plug away at a "regular" job to make them happy. But subscribing to the norm only works if that's how you're wired. Over the years, I've come to believe that my strong, independent, and entrepreneurial spirit may be a byproduct of my parents' courage to start anew in this country. Also, my parents once tried to open a Chinese restaurant and even though it failed, it taught me that it's better to chase your aspirations than live in regret.

## Saving Face

"Face" is how one is seen or judged by another in Asian cultures. Because of the Asian fixation on honor, we learn to do and achieve as a means to "save face." When people talk about how Asian cultures are shame-based, they're referring to the concern an Asian person has for what others think about him or her.

If someone "loses face," it creates a deep feeling of humiliation for letting down family, culture, and self. It should also be noted the Chinese character, or *kanji*, for "face" is the same as the character for "mask." If you follow this line of thinking, it's no wonder traditional Asians will do whatever it takes to hide their emotions by putting on their mask. Since saving face is seen as bringing honor to one's self and culture, then hiding one's true feelings also carries a degree of honor. But if you are to grow and heal from Asian cultural shame, you'll have to find another way to reframe your shame.

As a therapist, I have redefined shame in my own head. Instead of seeing it as a curse, it's now a blessing. I have insight that no therapy book could've given me when it comes to understanding addiction and recovery. I can walk and guide an addict toward recovery because I know firsthand the amount of patience, encouragement, and shame-reduction needed. Even if most of them do not know about my own journey, they may be able to sense a certain level of confidence and conviction in my voice when I give them feedback.

When I worked at the eating disorder clinic, I was shocked that so few therapists there had gone through therapy or had any firsthand knowledge of addiction or trauma. Clients would complain that therapists didn't treat them like real people. This is common when therapists don't do their own work. When we are too proud to undergo therapy ourselves, what does this communicate to clients? "I'm the healthy one; you're the one who's sick and in need of help." But in truth, we're all in need of help.

Due to their own lack of therapy, therapists may be "trauma-informed" (understand what trauma is, but not know how to work with a person's trauma). They may go too fast or they may never start at all. At the eating disorder clinic, clients would clamor and ask about having their trauma processed, only to hear that part of therapy gets referred out, since supervisors would discourage therapists from discussing trauma directly with clients, out of fear their symptoms would get worse. This is bad advice, similar to not talking about suicide with suicidal clients. If you want to truly heal someone, you can't be scared to talk about their issues. Asking a therapist what his or her beliefs are regarding therapy for him or herself may reveal all you need to know about whether the therapist is a good fit for you. I've heard stories from clients, especially minors, in which past therapists never talked to them about their parents' divorce or the abuse they endured, but simply played games with them because they were worried the client would get emotionally distraught. Talk about a bad therapeutic fit!

## The Nail that Sticks Up Gets Hammered Down

So what exactly is shame? Is it the same feeling as guilt? People often use guilt and shame interchangeably, but there is a distinction between the two that needs to be recognized if we are to understand the life-draining consequences of shame.

Guilt is healthy because it tells us what mistakes we need to correct and leads us to think of ways to reconcile our relationships with others. Healthy guilt is associated with feelings of remorse directed outwardly, toward another person. You think about how you have impacted another person's thoughts and feelings. There's a sense of constructive sorrow, and with it a love-motivated desire to change that is rooted in concern for others.

Shame, on the other hand, is a distorted belief that you are bad and unworthy of love. When a person feels shame, instead of focusing on correction, he or she focuses on self-persecution and punishment. Shame-based people believe their essential core is inherently defective and broken, which is reflected in their thoughts, beliefs, and behaviors that lack forgiveness and grace. In essence, guilt is our conscience telling us that we have failed and it moves us to change, whereas shame keeps us locked in a cycle of self-absorption and punishment. Clients display shame, for example, after disclosing their porn addiction to their partner. They will berate themselves with phrases like "I'm such a fuckup" or "I'm a bastard for doing what I've done." But in their self-loathing, they have a hard time empathizing with their partner's pain because they're too absorbed in their own shame. In my life, "I'm a bad boy" was the prevailing thought in childhood. "I should be punished." "God should strike me dead!" In therapy, guilt started taking hold. "I did some things I regret and now I can take responsibility and choose a different path."

## The Imposter Syndrome

By definition, an imposter is someone who practices deception under another character, name, or identity. There is a deep-seated belief that this person must hide his or her true self as a means to preserve filial honor. In more practical understanding, my Asian clients often feel like imposters because they are unwilling to break the Asian cultural standards and show their true feelings and emotions. They don't want to hide their faults and shortcomings. They don't want to lose their sense of self.

I've spent years feeling like an imposter myself. Even now sometimes I feel like a fraud as a therapist, since this is my second career. This is most likely to get triggered when I meet colleagues who say this was their calling for as long as they can remember. When I hear these stories I shrink. I feel less than. These same feelings took hold when I was in broadcasting. I always felt like an imposter, as my goal was never to work for CNN or some other major network doing "hard news." I wanted to do fluff pieces or human-interest stories for shows like *Entertainment Tonight* or *Access Hollywood*. Yet I dared not share those aspirations with others, lest I be viewed with less credibility.

This sense of feeling like I'm duping others started at a young age. I was an immigrant and not an American citizen, and that always nagged at my sense of worth and adequacy. I didn't want to be rejected, so I just blended in as much as I could. This imposter syndrome continued once my porn/sexual obsessions kicked in because I felt I had to present an image of perfection, especially in Asian-American Christian circles. This sense of inadequacy is the breeding ground for many clients I treat, regardless of the issues bringing them in.

When Asian clients come to counseling, generations of habits, thoughts, and beliefs follow them. One of the most pernicious is that these individuals believe they are not good enough and will never be good enough. They may have succeeded academically, professionally, or relationally by worldly standards, but there's a profound sense that deep down they are imposters, illegitimate beings who deserve to be found wanting. These distorted beliefs and perceptions gnaw at their soul.

It is not easy to unearth the truth, but with enough trust, honesty, and vulnerability built in the context of a therapeutic relationship, what seeps out is the acknowledgment that they can't continue being prisoners of their minds. In other words, they feel a sense of contempt and despair, as their image of perfection begins to crumble. But as the need to maintain Asian cultural honor slowly recedes, what grows in its place is the true self waiting to be seen, known, and loved unconditionally.

What's needed is an invitation to let them be. They desire to tap into their core beliefs, feelings, and fears within a safe relationship, be it a friend, family member, or therapist. As safety grows, so does the realization that they can live a new life free of these expectations. While some may need to switch careers or escape unhealthy relationships to free themselves from the cultural bind, most only need to be graced with affirmation that their truth matters. When an Asian person goes through life striving for acceptance through performance, they lose all sense of healthy relational recognition, which is one free of judgment.

The fear of abandonment that lies beneath the fear of being an imposter must be dismantled and replaced by the belief that they are loved and cherished for who they are rather than what they have achieved. They must be known not for their human accomplishments, but for simply being.

## 'They Did the Best They Could'

Most of my Asian clients repeatedly received messages that denied their feelings and invalidated their experiences. Some examples of these messages include "Stop feeling that way!" "How can you be tired; you haven't done anything!" and "You shouldn't be upset at your father. Look what he's done for you!"

In emotionally disconnected Asian families, when children express their thoughts and feelings, their parents dismiss them or belligerently shame them. Consistent invalidation over time has long-lasting consequences that I consider soul murder. As adults, these Asians enter therapy because they have lost their abilities to know what they want or like.

These clients tend to minimize the impact of their neglect and abuse. "All the Asian parents did the same thing as my family." "They provided for us, so I know they loved us." Or "My parents did the best they could." This defensive strategy is typical during the early stages of therapy. Love is viewed from their parents' intentions, no matter how abusive or damaging they were. Later these clients are more open to the idea that their parents may have tried their best to love them, but their actions could also be construed as abusive (emotionally, spiritually, or physically), whether intentional or otherwise.

Why is this so difficult for Asian clients to acknowledge in treatment? Part of the answer lies in the Asian collectivist mindset to honor your ancestors, elders, and parents above all else. This means that no word, deed, or gesture can be used to bring any form of negativity toward your parents. This message is underscored by immigrant Asian parents when they guilt-trip their children. The paradox and tension are even more apparent when clients defend or rationalize behaviors such as grabbing, yelling, hitting, or threatening abandonment. Once trust is developed, clients can see how abuse can and often does happen within "loving" and well-intentioned families.

Just because someone loves you doesn't mean it's a healthy relationship, free of abuse. Within traditional Asian households, physical or verbal abuse needs to be identified as a misguided form of love. Traditional Asian parents like to defend their actions as love, when they are actually more of a misguided interpretation of love in an attempt to discipline and teach their children.

I tell clients that abuse is abuse and needs to be acknowledged and understood so it doesn't carry over to the next generation. In those moments of validation and understanding, the space for true healing occurs. No longer do these clients turn a blind eye to the past, but they can grasp the uneasy reality that love and abuse can happen under the same roof.

## Asian Shame and Blame

The traditional Asian worldview is one where shame and blame are commonplace. I was reminded of that when I gave a personality test to measure an Asian client's level of empathy and came across a question to the effect of, "If a friend was ripped off by a con artist, how would you respond?" The client answered in a very traditional Asian way, "That person deserved it!" In American or Western psychological profiles, that would be deemed pathological, due to lacking empathy to another's plight. But Asians would counter that this is the epitome of empathy because by stating the person "deserved" to get ripped off they are thinking of how they would be helping another person avoid a similar situation (i.e. through the use of shame). My Asian-American clients report being on the receiving end of statements like the one above. Here are some examples:

- "John should just kill himself then!" (Parents' response when hearing their teenage son is depressed and having suicidal thoughts)

- "What's wrong with you? How can you be so clumsy?" (Parents' response to their son falling off a bike and getting hurt)

- "I warned her that was the wrong college major, but she was so stubborn and wouldn't listen." (Parents' response to their daughter struggling to find a job after graduating with a liberal-arts degree)

Part of the reason for these negative responses is the Asian cultural mandate of honor. When someone does anything that could be construed as shaming or dishonoring to the Asian family or culture, the typical response would be similar to the ones above.

One of the biggest barriers to healing is when Asian clients struggle to acknowledge the loss, grief, or feelings of hurt caused by their parents. Much of this is related to the belief that speaking about these issues is shaming their parents.

Early in my own therapy Dr. Steve asked about my family and the lack of childhood affirmation, touch, or any other explicit means of communicating love. I simply could not differentiate that speaking about the pain wasn't blaming them for it.

Yet with time I embraced the need to acknowledge the cultural and family struggles, leading to the beginning of my healing. The resentments began receding and empathy for my parents' own challenges helped me appreciate their shortcomings. Nowadays I have a richer appreciation of what my parents were going through, while also recognizing that they may have made some mistakes.

## Long Duck Dong and Western Beauty Collide

No discussion about Asian-Americans can avoid the subject of beauty and how it impacts the psyche of those who aren't subscribing to the standards of Western society. If you're Caucasian and lived in Asia, I doubt your self-esteem would be impacted to the point where you wanted to look more Asian in an attempt to fit in. I doubt you would get eyelid surgery or use creams to darken your skin. Yet double-eyelid surgery and whitening creams abound in Asian countries as a means to look more Western.

Specifically, when it comes to Asian women, small or flat breasts may impact their sense of femininity. My ex-wife struggled with accepting her breast size, so she purchased a $5,000 contraption that purportedly made her breasts larger by sucking out the air around them with a vacuum seal. Others have had breast-augmentation surgery.

Growing up in the eighties, my only reference point for masculinity was from what I learned in mainstream media and Hollywood. That didn't bode well for me, since Asian men were seen as emasculated, asexual, and undesirable. Dorks, nerds, or heavy-accented buffoons is how Hollywood has often portrayed Asian men. As a result, there were not a lot of positive role models for Asian men. Other kids would tease me mercilessly with broken English and make physical gestures to the racist chant of "Chinese, Japanese, dirty knees, look at these!" As I hit puberty, there were references and jokes about Asian penis size. I tried to tune it out, but it invariably made me wish I was anything but an Asian male. When women rejected me, the first thought was, Is it because I'm Asian? Or, Do they think I'm not man enough for them?

In the United States, masculinity and virility is rife with stereotypes and caricatures and deeply embedded in mainstream media messages. Consider the following: the Italian stallion, the Latin lover, the Black stud. All of these carry a hypersexual or overly sexualized perception of men from these various cultures. But the Asian male is relegated to the sphere of asexuality at best.

Part of this is due to the biased portrayals of Asian men in Hollywood. In the 1984 movie *Revenge of the Nerds*, the character Takashi is a Japanese nerd with a thick accent. To add insult to injury, he isn't even aware of what a nerd is, let alone that he was viewed as one. Ironically, the actor who played Takashi is a Japanese-American born in the United States, but he was cast to play the role of an immigrant who couldn't speak English well, let alone understand the cultural and sexual nuances of dating women in the U.S. (I always rooted for the "nerds," thinking if they were able to garner attraction from women, then maybe people like me also had a chance.)

Also released in '84, the popular coming-of-age comedy *Sixteen Candles* showcased the character Long Duk Dong, an Asian foreign-exchange student who was nerdy, horny, and emasculated. The sound of a gong reverberated whenever his character entered a scene. Alison MacAdam, a former NPR senior editor, said this about the legacy of the character, "The mark Long Duk Dong left was more of a stain: To some viewers, he represents one of the most offensive Asian stereotypes Hollywood ever gave America."

Dong's love interest in the movie is a woman much larger than him known as "Lumberjack," which further mocks the masculinity of Asian men. "The gender roles are switched," Kent Ono and Vincent Pham wrote in their book *Asian Americans and the Media*. "While this representation aims to provide comic relief, it both feminizes Asian American men and simultaneously constructs alternative gender and sexuality as aberrant."

The cofounders of the Asian-American popular culture magazine *Giant Robot*, Martin Wong and Eric Nakamura, said before *Sixteen Candles* students of Asian descent in the United States were often nicknamed "Bruce Lee." As recently as 2001, when I was working in Los Angeles, people called me "Bruce Lee" at the YMCA when I was playing pick-up basketball. It was infuriating that, in the twenty-first century, this was deemed acceptable.

After *Sixteen Candles*, Asian guys were nicknamed "Donger" after Long Duk Dong. Wong said, "If you're being called Long Duk Dong, you're comic relief amongst a sea of people unlike you." Nakamura said, "You're being portrayed as a guy who just came off a boat and who's out of control. It's like every bad stereotype possible, loaded into one character."

Long Duk Dong was played by a Japanese-American actor who was raised in the United States and did not have an accent. But the actor, Gedde Watanabe, won the role by posing as an immigrant who knew no English. In a 2014 interview with the online magazine *Vulture*, to commemorate the thirtieth anniversary of the movie, Watanabe explained, "To set myself apart, I asked a friend of mine who had a thick Korean accent if I could hang out with him and learn. I then went to the audition in character using my friend's accent. Which wasn't a very smart idea because I was basically lying and would have to tell them at some point that I only spoke English and was from Ogden, Utah."

In 2000, when Chinese martial arts actor Jet Li played the male lead in the film *Romeo Must Die*, the end scene initially had him kissing his co-star, played by the late African-American singer Aaliyah. The scene didn't test well with focus groups, which stated they were uncomfortable seeing an Asian man kissing a woman. The movie's director, Gene Cayhon, explained in an interview with the *Korea Times*, "Mainstream America, for the most part, gets uncomfortable with seeing an Asian man portrayed in a sexual light." The scene was changed to Aaliyah giving Jet Li a hug. Ugh! All of my Asian guy friends and I were so upset when we saw this.

While there are now Asian-American male actors playing more mainstream roles, the searing images of Asian men as sexually castrated loom large in the minds and perceptions of the American public and many women in the dating world.

These stereotypes, no doubt, played out in my own sexual behaviors. To combat this negative perception, I overcompensated and tried to prove to women that Asian men could be handsome, charming, and sexual and, in my case, even over-sexual.

My single, Asian, male clients complain to me about the dating scene. Some cite things like the 2014 OkCupid study that revealed Asian men were the least desirable in online dating preferences. Since then, other studies have revealed even more startling statistics. An American Sociological Association journal article titled "Asian American Men in Romantic Dating Markets," published in 2018, reported that more than 90 percent of non-Asian women said they would not date an Asian man and 40 percent of Asian women said they would not date an Asian man.

The contrast is stark compared to my white, male clients, who complain that they can't keep track of all the women reaching out to them via dating apps.

Not only do Asian men feel spurned by white women, they also, as the above statistic suggests, feel rejected by Asian women. Even Asian-American women have been indoctrinated into viewing Asian men as lacking romance and as sexually inert and thus unattractive. And this isn't just in the U.S.; it's an international issue.

In a February 2020 online article for The Conversation, "Asian Guys Stereotyped and Excluded in Online Dating," Dr. Yue Qian, an assistant professor of sociology at the University of British Columbia, recognized how significant this issue is after creating two profiles on a mainstream dating app: one of an Asian man and one of an Asian woman. However, to try to mitigate looks as an issue, she created profiles in which the pictures only showed the profile view of the prospective Asian man and woman, both of who were wearing sunglasses. The profiles had the same unisex name, "Blake," and the same interests and activities— for example, sushi and beer. According to the article, the female Blake got numerous "likes," "winks," and messages every day, whereas the male Blake got very little response.

This was an unscientific study, but it nevertheless confirms what many Asian men in the online dating world experience. In The Conversation article, one Filipino-Canadian man said he quit online dating out of frustration. "I don't like online anymore. It doesn't do you justice. Most women who I ask to date would be Caucasian and I would get a lot of 'no responses.' And if they did [respond to why they clicked 'no' on my profile] they say they were not attracted to Asian men. So in a sense, metaphorically, I didn't get a chance to bat. Because they look at my ethnicity and they say no."

While many people can and do find love online, Asian-American men clearly face significant challenges men of other ethnic backgrounds do not. It's not to say it's impossible, but the cultural hurdle is much higher and the wounds of rejection deeper. In the mental-health world, this can translate into a deep sense of inadequacy for some Asian men.

Some Asian men are so discouraged with dating that they've resigned themselves to porn. I've even had Asian male clients who specifically look at porn where the man is humiliated by another man, reflecting their own trauma (e.g. looking at porn where the storyline shows one man luring away another man's girlfriend and having sex with her). In therapy we call this "trauma re-enactment"—clients finding real or imagined scenarios that give them a sense of rejection or abuse, with the hopes of changing the storyline to heal themselves. But the healing doesn't occur because they put themselves in traumatic situations that have no way out. But once clients gain insight into their behaviors, change can happen because they now have awareness of the unconscious dynamics drawing them to their trauma bonds.

## No Kissing Rule and Other Asian Sexual Taboos

Asian cultures have a long history of sexual taboos. Kissing was viewed as taboo in parts of Asia as recently as the late nineteenth century, when an anthropologist observed that many Asian cultures viewed mouth-to-mouth kissing as an "abomination." In Japan, kissing on the mouth was considered to be as intimate as having sex, relegated to the privacy of the bedroom. Thus, many Europeans visiting the country assumed the Japanese didn't kiss. As late as the 1930s, kissing in public was viewed as shocking.

If kissing was once considered taboo, you can imagine how taboo it is to talk about sex and sexual struggles. If young Asians do hear anything about sex, it is usually presented as abhorrent, unless it's confined to a loving, marital relationship. You can probably see how this creates a shame-filled trap for those struggling with sexual behaviors. If young people are discouraged from talking about their sexual struggles, they may see themselves and their behaviors as "dirty."

Regardless of ethnicity or culture, a heavy cloak of shame covers those mired in a web of sexual affairs, obsessions, and addictions. Whether it's cybersex, casual sex, pornography, prostitutes, or compulsive masturbation, the combined feelings of dirtiness, defectiveness, and weakness all race to the forefront. When shame ensnares a person, that individual develops an intrinsic feeling of being unlovable, worthless, and a failure, fueling the insidious cycle of shame and addiction.

From an addict's perspective, to be weak and powerless is the ultimate humiliation. After years of seeming self-sufficiency, the addict's acknowledgment that something else (i.e. substances or behaviors) controls him or her is demoralizing. It's difficult to admit to ourselves, our families, and our loved ones that we need help. A true addict simply can't recover on one's own power. Acknowledging this prepares addicts for the road to recovery. In twelve-step recovery meetings, addicts recognize the first step is when they learn to break their denials and excuses by acknowledging their powerlessness over the addiction and that they need to depend on others for help. They come to a point of brokenness where they realize they cannot control everything in their lives and they must surrender that control. However, before an addict can accept this reality or epiphany, he or she usually has experienced years of getting stuck in the cycle of shame and addictive behaviors.

## Intimacy Is Possible

I know from my own addiction that recovery is not only possible but life-enriching. It's more than just sobriety from a behavior. It's also about living an authentic and transparent life. I no longer live with the fear of intimacy with others that initially drove me to pornography. I do not hide my feelings from others or myself.

I am able to be vulnerable, knowing this will build relationships rather than fearing abandonment from them.

This has been a long but steady process spanning twenty years. Much of the time has been invested in therapy, but also in personal growth and exploration. This means when I cut out my addiction, I was able to discover new interests that make me come alive, including photography and poetry. Others are more visceral, such as swimming or riding my motorcycle. Contemplation and reflection away from distractions are the key. I go on vacation or use other avenues to ensure I am not distracted by my smartphone or computer. My body is also a source of knowledge. Early in recovery, I put a lot of emphasis on finding insight into my thoughts. Now I focus on what my body is telling me. The various sensations that come up give me clues to what I like and don't like and allow me to be more attuned to my entire self. If I notice my chest tightening or heart racing, I pause, knowing my body is alerting me that I am getting triggered.

Being more present is the ideal. My addictive brain wants to live in fantasy, either in the past or daydreaming about the future. I work hard to stay grounded to my surroundings and feelings. If I notice myself getting distracted or dissociating from a situation, I make note of it so I can be more aware in the future.

What I've learned from this long journey is that the wounds from one's past are real and must be dealt with if one is suffering. These wounds cannot simply be dismissed. The core pangs of our hearts can drive us to fill the hole with not just addictions but other things that aren't viewed as negatively by society. Food, material goods, work, excessive exercise, and a plethora of other normal, everyday activities can be used as a barrier in relationships. The loss, hurt, and need to hide and numb out must all be processed so one can grieve and grow into emotional and spiritual maturity. What is the deep disappointment within your soul? How have you used this pain to justify or rationalize past or current behaviors? How would it feel to be stripped of your need for control?

That is the ultimate test: How to surrender the need for control and autonomy? How to trust the process? There's no one, magical way to recover, but those in recovery know the first step is critical: having the humility to finally acknowledge you have a problem and sharing it with someone else. Addicts need to move beyond the cycle of acting out (i.e. using their drug of choice), suffering in silence, and going through the repeat cycle of shame and addiction. They need to take the relational risk of vulnerability so they can heal and have their feelings and concerns validated, as well as being challenged to see beyond themselves and their impact on others.

## The Spiritual Journey Home

Self-awareness is great. Therapy is healing. Accountability is helpful. But nothing will break an addiction unless there's an understanding that life is a spiritual journey. Spiritual also has a broader meaning, as it addresses areas of life that many addicts struggle with, such as forgiveness (of themselves and others), loving oneself, accepting responsibility, and honestly grieving areas of their lives where there's been relational hurt, disappointment, or betrayal. Spiritual growth encompasses so many areas beyond just stopping a behavior. Instead of abject anxiety, despair, hopelessness, or fear, these crippling emotions get replaced by serenity, peace, and a deep-seated knowledge that you're going to be okay.

Spirituality is also learning to develop a new relationship with our shared humanity and addictions. The addictions must be seen as a false security blanket for emotional intimacy and refuge. To take these addictions off center stage, we must surrender them to the universe. Only when these areas get developed do addicts stand a chance at real change and transformation. I believe everything about the recovery process should be considered spiritual or soul work. We must learn to commit to a community where we are known, seen, understood, accepted, yet also challenged to do better.

Community also provides accountability that can come in the form of a mentor, another addict in recovery, therapist, or friend. Verbalizing our ever-changing emotional needs and concerns to people whom you respect and are in regular contact with is essential. Isolation and secrecy are where addictions and shame thrive. Thwarting them requires courageous conversations.

Broadly speaking, people are vulnerable to addictions when there's unresolved trauma in their lives. Trauma is more than just physical or sexual abuse. It can come from emotional neglect. A mother or father may have been physically unavailable. It can be a pattern of put-downs. All of these examples can be traumatic if the circumstances result in the belief that one cannot trust others with one's internal world. Part of therapy is helping clients process the deep, childhood trauma that drove them to find comfort in whatever compulsive or addictive behavior they've grown dependent on.

## Be Broken and Be Proud

Those dealing with addictions, shame, trauma, or significant loss can feel broken, inadequate, and worthless. But there's another way to feel about yourself: Be proud of your brokenness, knowing that it can be redeemed for the greater good. When you enter your wound, you will discover your true glory. In his book *Iron John*, Robert Bly says, "Where a man's wound is, that is where his genius will be."

The wound gives us humility and makes us more real to those around us, instead of trying to prop ourselves up with our own ego and self-serving desires, ambitions, talents, and accomplishments. Our brokenness also offers us a glimpse of what we can offer the world, if we're willing to listen to the call.

It's ironic how true this is for me. As a first-generation Chinese immigrant, I was indoctrinated to bring honor to my family and ancestry while chasing the American dream. But it wasn't until that dream of success, perfection, and self-reliance was obliterated that I had the courage to delve deep into my own wounds of cultural shame and addiction. Only then was I able to find what I was looking for in life: meaning, passion, purpose, and an unswerving desire to help others dealing with shame, addictions, trauma, or a sense of self.

I no longer see my faults as bringing shame to my family, my culture, or myself. Instead, my faults are a chance to showcase the power of grace—grace that makes good out of our trials and disappointments. It's this belief that our shattered dreams can bring forth a new promise, hope, and way of living that propels me. Despite moments of debilitating fear, humiliation, and hopelessness, know that no matter how desperate the situation, therein lies the greatest opportunity for spiritual growth and discovery.

## America: The Land of Second Chances

If it was ever misunderstood from this book or from my experiences, I want it to be unequivocally clear: I love the United States. My family loves this country. Despite the challenges, it gave my parents the opportunity to start anew and reinvent themselves.

I got a second chance, too, here in America. If I was in Hong Kong, I'm sure the shame of my addiction would've stayed underground. There wouldn't be an opportunity for redemption. But Americans are more open and forgiving. While they love to see the mighty fall, they also love a good comeback story. Regardless of the circumstances, if you're willing to acknowledge your faults and take accountability, there's room for mercy and grace. I'm thankful for this.

On my journey of healing here in Seattle, I was able to get remarried and become the father of a spirited boy. I now have the family I've always wanted. Along with having a wife and child,

I'm able to be emotionally connected to them. This would never have been possible in my earlier years when I was checked out of relationships. When I was in the throes of my addiction, I had no headspace for anything but my own wants and needs. I couldn't truly empathize with others or think about their needs.

In my new family, I'm able to create a different narrative for myself and hopefully change the course of the generational patterns of addiction that plagued my family line dating back at least three generations. Having knowledge in therapy is a good foundation, but I also do my best to practice it with my family. Some of it is easy and fun, such as loving our child and demonstrating it through verbal praise and physical affection. Austin, who is seven years old, loves hugs and kisses. My wife and I also validate his interests. He's a creative child who enjoys making bracelets and drawing. He looks to us for simple encouragement and validation: "Mom and dad, look at this!" And we'd respond with "Great job!" or "I see that!" I estimate that by the time Austin was in kindergarten we had validated him on thousands of occasions. This is in stark contrast to our childhoods. (My wife is also Asian-American.) Now it makes sense why I looked for external validation through performance (academic or athletic) and porn.

The beauty of parenting, however, lies not in being reminded of the painful past but in the ability to re-parent ourselves through our children. Our losses in childhood can be healed, as we pour love into our children. I can love Austin as I wanted to be loved. This can also happen with our romantic partners. Through my current wife, I have learned to accept my divorce in a new way. I failed in my first marriage by staying silent and keeping my addiction a secret, and I ensured that didn't happen again when I met my wife. On our first few dates, the conversation steered toward past relationships. We had mutual friends, but Kathy didn't know anything about my past. I talked about my divorce, but also took another step of vulnerability: I shared that my addiction was one of the reasons for the divorce. Instead of rejection, there was understanding from her. Instead of judgment, there was curiosity.

My wife also accepts my creative, non-traditional lifestyle as a therapist. This isn't easy for her, as she comes from a traditional upbringing where her father was the breadwinner. In our relationship, she brings home the bacon and I joke that "I bring home the turkey bacon." Most of our friends work traditional, full-time jobs, so I stick out like a sore thumb, and her willingness to embrace my occupation and lifestyle is a blessing.

We have been together for nearly ten years, and occasionally my past trauma of rejection resurfaces and I'll say, "Just divorce me!" In those moments, she waits for me to calm down and points out that she's not going anywhere. She married me and is committed to me, regardless of how irrational I may get at times. Her commitment to me helps me stay committed to myself.

In my work as a therapist, there is no regular client load and no measure of completion. It can feel like an ongoing series of "to be continued." This, at times, can be discouraging, but my wife reminds me of the progress I have made and what I have accomplished. I've stayed committed to my therapy practice because of her, but also because I know I need to do this. I need to help spread this message of hope from one person to another. Cultural shame, addiction, racism, and trauma are real aspects of my life experiences as a first-generation, Chinese immigrant to America. Yet through it all, with the courage to heal, a new way of living is possible. My hope is that others will find their own courage to heal and, in doing so, also find their true voice and authentic self.

# Acknowledgments

This book has been a labor of love forged in pain and cultural shame. My story of immigration, acculturation, addiction, and relational loss didn't feel noteworthy to share with others. Yet, through time and connections with people along the journey, I was supported to get this message out.

I want to give credit to those whom without their support and guidance this book would not have been possible. First and foremost, to Central Recovery Press for publishing not only this book but specifically wanting to find and publish stories related to mental health and addiction recovery. My editor, Matthew O'Brien, who worked tirelessly and patiently through several revisions to help sculpt and craft my story in a way that only a talented editor like himself could do.

All my past therapists who have guided me along the path of healing and those that continue to hold me accountable and challenge me to be a better husband, father, and friend.

To John Kim for being an inspiration to me with your humor and creativity. Our time as roommates together in Los Angeles was a vital period when our vision of helping others was birthed.

To my wife and son whom I cherish for providing me new ways to help me change old habits. And ultimately to God for whom all things are possible.

Printed in the USA
CPSIA information can be obtained
at www.ICGtesting.com
JSHW022250180324
59449JS00005B/16

9 781949 481686